A Structure for *Spirit*

A Structure for *Spirit*

How to Create a Daily Practice

Karen Chrappa

BALBOA
PRESS

A DIVISION OF HAY HOUSE

Balboa Press books may be ordered through booksellers or by contacting:

Balboa Press
A Division of Hay House
1663 Liberty Drive
Bloomington, IN 47403
www.balboapress.com
1-(877) 407-4847

Because of the dynamic nature of the Internet, any web addresses or links contained in this book may have changed since publication and may no longer be valid. The views expressed in this work are solely those of the author and do not necessarily reflect the views of the publisher, and the publisher hereby disclaims any responsibility for them.

ISBN: 978-1-4525-3393-3 (sc)
ISBN: 978-1-4525-3394-0 (e)

Library of Congress Control Number: 2011910839

Any people depicted in stock imagery provided by Thinkstock are models, and such images are being used for illustrative purposes only.
Images provided by Don Myer

Certain stock imagery © Thinkstock.

Printed in the United States of America

Balboa Press rev. date: 7/18/2011

Dedication

Dear Pachamama~
Thank you for claiming me as a daughter of the Earth,
revealing to me your magic and mystery.
Thank you for informing me with the ways of the ancient,
for opening my eyes to your beauty and wonder.
Thank you for transforming me with your ways of healing,
your enduring compassion and immeasurable love.
Thank you for cleansing me with the grace of your waters,
carrying my sorrows and fears to your seas.
Thank you for holding my prayers in your soil,
to nurture and seed the blossoming of me.

Above to the Apus, the Sun, Moon and Stars~
Keepers of wisdom through time and through space,
thank you for reflecting your majesty in me.
Your visions inform me through lagoons of clear waters,
through magic and wonder you speak to me.
To Eagle who soars amidst the peaks of your mountaintops,
carrying my prayers so they may take flight.
Thank you for guiding my path on this Earth,
to discover the beauty and wisdom in me.

~HEYA OM~

In Memory of My Father,
RICHARD CHRAPPA
April 21, 1936 - July 14, 2010

Contents

Preface

After an extremely hot sweat lodge in the middle of August, I laid on the belly of Mother Earth after ceremony. Never had I felt held in such compassion, her cool soil a balm to my baking body. In that moment I made a promise. I would let everyone know the beauty of Pachamama. This is that promise fulfilled.

I do not offer this journal as some authority on how to be spiritual. I am not an enlightened being or guru. I am not a scholar or expert in the ways of theology or religion. I do not consider myself a writer. Why then write this journal? For me, it is a call from my soul, on a path of devotion, to be of service. What I can attest to with authority is the medicine that comes with a daily practice.

There are many paths to follow on the road to liberation. Each spiritual tradition has its own unique road map, its own unique voice. In the midst of these differences in path, a consistent thread weaves through. For wherever you travel, wherever you search, you are always guided to the road within. As much as we long to find truth out there, eventually we must surrender to the path within.

Our western mindset does not understand the value in devoting time each day to this inner journey. Although I had practiced yoga, and attempted meditation on and off since the early 80's, it was not until 1997 that a daily practice was imposed through a yoga therapy training I was in. A few times a week was the usual time I devoted to practice, but every day? I resisted; heavily. Each morning an arduous battle raged between the countless reasons to stay in bed or the choice to get up and sit with myself.

The mandatory time requirement for the daily practice lasted six months. As time passed, resistance ebbed. A daily practice took root and became integral to my life. My daily practice, more than any other action I have taken in my life, accelerated my own spiritual evolution. This journal is a path woven from a dedication to practice, offering guidance and support, so you may realize the benefits and blessings that come with a daily practice. The benefits of practice do not come from reading about practice. The benefits come only with practice. This journal offers the experience of a daily practice regardless of whether you have had a practice before.

A daily practice is medicine for your soul. So much of your time and attention is spent each day on the necessary and mundane aspects of your life. You devote time to paying bills, buying groceries, tending to family, doing laundry, and never mind the endless demands of work and making a living. You lose sight of your soul, cannot hear your own heart, because there is no time devoted to listen.

One of the deepest acts of self-love is the gift of a daily practice. It allows you to slow down, pay attention and hear the longings that whisper within. In the beginning, you identify your spiritual self as the one who sits, practices yoga, prays in the morning. With time and attention, your practice feeds your sacred essence. The voice of your heart and soul are fortified. The wisdom that shines through your practice touches all parts of your life. There is no distinction between your spiritual self and that which is not. You begin to bring the sacred to all aspects of your life, including time spent grocery shopping;, paying bills and all that is mundane.

A spiritual practice sees you through times of turmoil, takes you on a path from darkness to light. Through practice you cultivate the stillness of mind, the ease in heart and the wisdom of soul so your life becomes prayer, your heart is an offering and your path is one of communion with all that is.

Acknowledgments

I honor Spirit, for providing me with the inspiration, the perseverance and the synchronistic guidance to create and share this medicine.

Deep thanks to my dear friend, Stephanie Lipsey, a gifted writer and wise soul, who from the inception of this journal five years ago, has been a consistent, enthusiastic and inspirational support.

Thank you to my sisters in blood and Spirit, Kristine Chrappa, Michele Chrappa-Potkin, Lilyan Chrappa-Spoole, Tracy Warzer, Mary-Beth Charno, Karen Meyer and Stephanie Lipsey who

so willingly and warmly embraced this work and were among the first to step into this process.

Thank you to the countless patients and clients I have worked with over the decades that provided a depth of life experience and have continually inspired me on a healing path.

For Don Myer, a man who opened my heart to depths of love and who, through the ways of mystery, brought this journal to depths of wisdom it would not have known otherwise. His beauty is woven through this work through the stunning images that grace the cover and pages of this book.

Thank you to Judy Bath, a mentor extraordinaire, who I had the great fortune to meet in Peru, and who held the space for me to visit some of the darkest places within myself, thereby recovering the light of wisdom.

Thank you to Abhita Austin, a woman of passion, whose talents in sound and engineering patiently helped me create the guided meditations so essential to this process. Thank you to Kevin Macleod whose range of musical talent and creativity provide the perfect backdrop to each guided process.

I honor the ancestors of my blood and the lineage of Earthkeepers of Peru who have shown the way through the footsteps they have laid, illuminating a path of wisdom for each one of us to walk.

Thank you to my daughters, Sarabeth and Danielle, for giving me the greatest gift of being their mother.

I honor my mother and father for the grace that brought me into the world. For my mother, who has always held her family in the dedicated depths of her heart. My deepest thanks are offered to my Aunt Eileen whose light was the grace in my childhood. My deep appreciation is held for my family who has so unwaveringly offered their encouragement, guidance and support through all the endeavors of my life.

Guidelines for Using this Book

- This journal provides a structure to create a daily practice, supported by guided meditations available by download for $9.99 at www.karenchrappa.com. They are essential to this process.

- There are eight guided meditations of approximately ten to fifteen minutes in length. Starting on Day 4 you will be instructed to follow one a day as part of your daily practice. Try to create time for this in the morning, even if it means waking a bit earlier. It will help set a tone for your day. Feel free to listen to any of the guided practices more often if you like.

- There is one guided shamanic journey. This journey is taken on Day 2 to meet a Spirit ally. Your Spirit ally will serve as s source of guidance and wisdom during this process and beyond.

- Establishing time each day to turn your attention inside develops clarity and insight, fortifies and builds confidence in your spiritual self. Create an inviting space in your home to come to your practice each day. The space need not be elaborate or large. A simple cushion or seat is enough.

- I encourage attention to this process every day; however do not despair if you miss a day. Keep going. Thirty days of the process may take 45 days or more to complete. That is OK. What is more important is to complete the journal, no matter how long it takes. Keep coming back; start where you left off, as often as you need.

- This journal is a course in the study of self. Awareness is created through a variety of guided practices. As your awareness heightens, everything you do becomes an opportunity to see your patterns, habits and behaviors more clearly, not just during the guided process. Watch how you approach this journal. Do you need to know everything before you start? Do you prejudge or criticize the process thereby discarding it all together? Do you put off getting started or start with great enthusiasm then fade, unable to complete the process? Do you feel you know everything already? Notice how your approach to this journal is how you approach other aspects of your life.

- If you have resistance to getting started, try listening to *Attitude of Gratitude*, the *Body Scan* or *Heart of Peace* to test the waters. Listen before going to sleep at night to re-inform you during dreamtime.

- This journal starts with intention. If you are having difficulty setting an intention, do not let that stop you from getting started. Let your intention be to create clarity or to discover an intention for yourself. Notice if a desire to have everything perfect or just right keeps you from beginning this journal. How does that pattern show up in other aspects of your life? Where else do you keep yourself from starting something new?

- Be kind to yourself during this process. If you miss a day, notice if your tendency is to criticize or condemn yourself. Does missing a day mean you can't complete the journal or you have failed in some way? Watch your own patterns of flexibility or rigidity during this process. This is offered to support you and its intention is to enhance, not hinder, the relationship with yourself.

- At the end of each day you are asked to list 5 things you are grateful for. This keeps your attention on the blessings and abundance that already exist. Use the blank pages at the end of the book if more room is needed for writing.

- Prepare for each day by reading the journal entry the night before or first thing in the morning.

- As with any practice, the benefits of the guided meditations go deeper the more you use them. I encourage you to listen as often as you like, and to continue even once you complete the journal.

- While using this journal include some attention to your body. This process will begin to shift blockages in your system. Movement, exercise or massage are all effective methods for supporting your body. Walking in nature is highly recommended if possible. Yoga, tai chi, dance, even making love more often would all be wonderful ways to assist your body in moving energy through your system.

To support you in your daily practice,
download the Shamanic Journey and Guided Meditations at:

www.karenchrappa.com
Available for $9.99

Recorded at Hidden Chapel Studios by Abhita Austin
Music by Kevin MacLeod www.incompetech.com

Tracks Include:

"Knowing yourself

is the beginning of all wisdom."

BUDDHA

Setting Intention

Your intention is a crystallization of thought, energy and awareness in a specific direction to create your desire. Everything in your life has been created this way, starting as a thought, charged with feeling, and manifesting into your world, whether you are aware of it or not. To create your life with consciousness, you must be willing to look with brutal honesty at what your life is reflecting back to you. If your life is one of lack, then lack resides somewhere in you. If your life is one of limitation, then that limitation lives within. If your relationships are deficient in love, where is it you do not love yourself?

To create a life you desire starts with awareness. Becoming aware of what you want is important, but equally important is becoming aware of wounds, unresolved feelings and the painful past

that are creating and informing your life right now, providing obstacles to that which you seek. We develop sophisticated and elaborate strategies to avoid and hide from these places within. We live under the illusion that what we don't see will go away. The painful truths we run and hide from in ourselves do not go anywhere. They live on within us, hiding in shadows, informing and shaping the life we are living like a trickster, beyond the sight of our very own awareness. To create a life you desire, you must bring awareness to what you want to create, as well as bring awareness to what is getting in the way. This is the adventure you will embark on through this journal.

The process of manifesting dwells in the realms of mystery. When you consciously step into creating intentions for yourself, you are co-creating with the Universe, or Spirit, or Divine Intelligence, or God or whatever name you would like to use for that which is beyond naming. Co-creating with Spirit attracts opportunities that you could not have invoked on your own. Possibilities exist where there were none before. Obstacles are lifted, pathways created. You tap into a synchronistic realm that is beyond reason. The less your intention is burdened with your own personal agenda and direction, the greater the power for Spirit to work through you. If certainty, safety, fact and logic have been the tools you have relied on to navigate your way through life, conscious co-creation will challenge the foundation on which you have built your beliefs.

Cultivating a relationship with Spirit is not a one-way path where you ask for what you want and all is provided for. As with every relationship, the relationship with Spirit calls for reciprocity and mutual exchange. For your part, you are called to shed many things that have gotten in the way of this conscious creative process. You are asked to let go of expectations, let go of how you think things should go, let go of the idea that you have control over events or people in your life. You are asked to stop blaming others for your own misery. You are asked to step into the flow of mystery. You are challenged to become comfortable with not knowing. In this process of creative co-creation you are asked to cultivate faith, to cultivate trust. You are asked to fortify confidence in your spiritual self. When you begin to trust your higher self, you come to know the ways of magic.

As your intention is born, obstacles to that intention must die. This great cycle of life and death moves you through the time and space of your life. The largest cycle occurs between your first inhalation as you enter the world and your last exhalation as you leave. Yet within this large circle of your life and death cycle, occur many small cycles of varying degrees and intensities of this very same process.

We have all felt death to some degree in our life, whether it was through the loss of a loved one, the loss of a job, the loss of a relationship or losing something we value like our home. With every death comes an opportunity for something new to be born. How many times can you look back on what appeared to be a hardship in your life, only to discover the blessings, the gifts and the wisdom that was gained through those experiences?

If you are looking to create joy, then your sadness and sorrow must be put to rest. If you would like to create a new future, then you must stop clinging to your past. If you want to create abundance then every part of yourself that says I am not enough must go.

As you embark on this journey, you will begin to develop a greater awareness of what is getting in the way of what you desire. What fears, limited beliefs and self-sabotaging patterns exist that need to be shed? Letting go can be where the greatest difficulty arises. The tools and techniques, along with the guided meditations, will begin to cultivate a greater capacity to see with more clarity, where you have created obstacles. From that place of awareness, true change can come about. As these old, outdated patterns reconfigure, people, situations and events in your life shapeshift as well. The benevolence of creation is always nudging you toward your light, through this cycle of life and death.

As for the specifics of setting an intention, simplicity is best. The first practice in the book is about setting your intention. What would you like to call into your life? What would you like to cultivate? What are you ready to step into? You may already know what that it is, but if not, you can look at your life and see what is not working as a way to know what would serve you.

There may be fear about money, resources or job issues, rooted in a sense of lack. Rather than set an intention about wanting a certain amount of money or getting a specific job, let your intention be one of ABUNDANCE. Allow abundance to begin to inform your life. The demands of your life may weigh heavily on your time and health, leaving you overwhelmed and stressed. An intention could be to SIMPLIFY or cultivate BALANCE. An intention of OPTIMUM HEALTH or VITALITY may serve you. What would it feel like to live from that place in your life?

Perhaps you are not sure what your intention is. Maybe you are full of confusion and doubt. Set an intention of calling forth CLARITY or CLEAR VISION. Are you able to stand up for yourself, say no and create boundaries? Call forth SELF NURTURING, SELF CARE or SELF WORTH. Do you value yourself? Do you need to claim your right to be here? Set an intention of stepping into your POWER or BEAUTY or hold the intention of I AM. Do you procrastinate and put things off? Set an intention of FORTITUDE.

In this process of setting intention, distill what you are looking to create into its most fundamental essence. See if your intention can be set with one word. Let this be the step on which your journey begins.

DAY 1

DATE _____

INTENTIONS

*"Let yourself be silently drawn
by the stronger pull of what you really love."*
RUMI

1. Today you will set an intention for what you would like to create in your life. You can ask what would you like to receive or call into your life? Where would you like to create change? Are there issues that are weighing heavily in your life that are causing distress? What would you like to step into?

2. Take a moment to reflect on what you feel is not working in your life. List all the things you are not happy with, areas where you feel stuck, places that feel they will never change. Reflect on all aspects of your life as you do this: relationships, family, work, health, money, life purpose. Write your list here.

3. From this list of what is not working, notice what is causing the most distress for you. Is it unhappiness or dissatisfaction with work or relationships? Is there a lack of purpose or meaning in your life? Are you living in fear of not having enough money or resources? Does your life feel overwhelming, out of balance or stuck? Are you facing a health crisis? Do you live with chronic pain? As you feel and sense this distress in your life, notice how that feels in your body. Close your eyes as you sense any areas that feel tight or clenched? Do you notice anxiety or uneasiness? Are there places within that feel as if they are holding on or gripping? What does your overall mental and emotional state feel like as you call to mind this distress? Write what you notice in your body here.

4. If you were living without this distress, what might your life feel like? Close your eyes and notice how this feels. Do you sense any subtle shifts or changes in how your body feels as you move from thinking about the distress to imagining your life without the distress? Write what you notice here.

5. As you reflect on your insights from above, what would you like to create? What would you like to receive? What would you like to call into your life? Who are you ready to step into becoming? What parts of yourself are you ready to reclaim? How do you want to walk through your life? What is at the essence of what you are seeking? Write your reflections here.

6. As you reflect on the answers from the question above, begin to simplify. Distill their essence into one or two words to create your intention for your life at this moment. Write your intention here.

7. At some point today find two stones that fit comfortably in the palm of your hand. One you will use during your shamanic journey, the other will hold your intention and be released.

8. With one of your stones, hold your intention as a thought. Breathe deeply into what you are feeling, thinking and sensing in your body in response to your intention. With a strong exhalation, blow what you are feeling and sensing from your body into one of the stones. Your breath energetically transfers your intention to this element of nature. You will then return this stone to the elements. If you live near a natural body of water, you can release it there. You can bury it in the Earth. This is your first step in releasing your intention and your attachment to its outcome. It begins your conversation with Spirit, your step into the realm of mystery, beyond the dimensions of your rational mind.

9. The other stone will be used on your shamanic journey tomorrow. Cleanse the stone in a sea salt bath before your journey. Further instructions regarding the stone and your journey will follow.

10. List 5 things you are grateful for today.

Spirit Ally

An ally is one who has your best interests at heart, someone on your side, a voice you trust as you seek guidance or direction. More often that not, the voice you hear, the one that guides the direction of your life, is the voice of fear, the voice of lack, the voice of doubt, the voice of self hatred.

The inner voices you have come to rely on for direction are the ones that say you are not enough. The ones that tell you can't do that. You'll never make it. You'll never have enough money. Where did you get that idea? What good are you? Who do you think you are anyway? These voices become what you hold as true about yourself. They shape your identity, how you see yourself, how you interact with others and the world. They are the voices that are attracting circumstances and people to you while they create your life. These are the voices that have become your allies.

Even if these voices steer you in the opposite direction by creating the mindset, "I'll show you", they are still driving your life out of spite and contempt. These voices consume your precious life energy, as you find yourself caught in an internal battle of wills.

You long to be happy. You long to be loved. Yet these voices steer your life based on fear and limitation. They drive you along paths of pain and lack. It makes no sense to create a life of suffering. Why then follow the critic within? In the midst of pain, these allies offer security. They tell you something you already know. They allow you to cling to something with certainty, shield you in protection from the unknown. The familiar voice of misery, devoted and loyal, has been your companion for so very long. Without this ally, who then to rely on? Not knowing the outcome is too terrifying alone.

An ally in Spirit is a sacred companion. You discover a voice that sees your life from a higher perspective, beyond the familiar pathways of mind. When you heed the call of a Spirit ally, your life steps forth in a new direction, a sacred voice that speaks to your soul.

Through the shamanic journey, you come to meet your ally in Spirit. During this journey you access information from realms beyond your ordinary state of awareness, a realm rich in symbolism and divine wisdom. You begin to cultivate a relationship with an ally that recognizes you as Spirit, a source you can turn to for guidance in shaping a life of your highest calling. Living from this perspective gives your life richness and meaning as you come to see yourself as the sacred being that you are.

From this perspective you come to know that everything that happens has meaning. You move away from labeling this as good and that as bad. You begin to see beauty in the pain and the ecstasy, the darkness and the light. You see how everything is necessary, everything has its place and everything is sacred. You come to know that every thread of your experience creates the fabric that weaves together the majestic tapestry of your own life.

SHAMANIC JOURNEY

"Faith is daring the soul to go beyond what the eyes can see."
WILLIAM NEWTON CLARK

1. Today you will journey to meet a source of sacred wisdom from Spirit. The guided journey will take about 20 minutes. You also need time and space to write about your experience once you are done. Allow about 10 minutes for this. Do not rush yourself through this process. I do not suggest taking the journey and running out to start your day. Find time that allows for some space.

2. Guided instructions are on the audio file, Shamanic Journey. Instruction is offered here to prepare you for what you will need and what to expect. Create a time and space that is private and free from distraction, especially if you live with others. The journey will take place while you lie on your back so find a space that offers comfort. You may want to cover yourself in a blanket to ensure warmth. Make sure your space is dark or dimly lit. You can cover your eyes with a bandana, blindfold, eye pillow or small towel. The stone that you found and bathed in sea salt will be placed in your left hand during your journey.

3. The purpose of this journey is to meet a Spirit ally that will serve as a source of wisdom and guidance for you. Your ally may appear in many different forms on your journey. Your Spirit ally may be in human form and appear as an elder, a young child, a warrior, a priestess. Your ally may be an angelic being or fairy. An animal is a common ally. An object such as a crystal, sword, flower or wand may be your ally. You may be guided to a sacred site in nature such as a mountain, river, lagoon or tree for wisdom. These are offered as a few ideas of how an ally may appear however something completely different may show up and that is fine too. What is most important is that you trust your impressions, trust what you find, even if it appears to make no sense. We often second-guess our own intuitive nature. You may be holding expectations of visions of grandeur on your journey when the most humble gift can offer profound wisdom.

4. Track 1 will guide you through this process into a state of non-ordinary reality by starting with a simple breathing exercise. Let go of any expectations of what you think your journey should look like. There is no need to fear anything. You are not going under hypnosis or

losing control of your senses. You enter a very powerful state of perception where you receive information from dimensions of higher intelligence and awareness. Although you are in control of your journey, it is important to let go of control of guiding this process. Allow images or impressions to arise. It may take some time before you sense anything. Trust, relax and enjoy the process. Know that at anytime, for any reason, if you would like to stop your experience, simply open your eyes.

5. If you are not able to take this journey today due to schedule or time constraints in your day, plan to take the journey at another time soon. You want to complete this journey before going further with the journal. Note when you will be able to complete this here.

6. If you do not see anything on your journey, do not despair. You can come back and take the journey another time. If you have never journeyed before, apprehension, or a sense of not knowing what to expect may have gotten in the way of receiving information. Being more relaxed the second or third time around may help you access information from the conscious dream state induced by the journey.

7. You may not literally "see" on your journey. Notice information other than visual images, such as feelings, knowings, a felt sense of something. Your expectations about what you will see may be getting in the way of "seeing" information from other sources. "Seeing" happens through the eyes of your heart as you journey rather than through the eyes of your mind. You may dismiss information that does not appear in a way you consider "seeing." Drop your attention from the eyes of your mind to the eyes of your heart to receive information through all your senses, from all levels of perception. Maybe you experience smells, tactile or body sensations. Notice everything on your journey.

8. Your Spirit ally can offer wisdom and guidance that can last your lifetime or your Spirit ally may be with you for a short time. Trust they will serve you for as long as needed. There is no specific time this will last.

9. Your stone that you use during your journey energetically holds the information from your Spirit ally. Tonight you can begin to ask the stone to inform you during dreamtime. Keep your stone in your left hand, your receptive channel, through the night. Use a sock or glove to hold it in place. Ask for the information from your journey to inform and guide you.

10. Tomorrow you will create an altar for your Spirit ally to honor and hold them sacred. An altar is another way to cultivate this relationship. Instruction for this will be given on Day 3 of the journal.

11. List 5 things you are grateful for today. Include your Spirit ally.

Shamanic Journey Reflections

A Shamanic Perspective

You can use the shamanic journey at other times, with a different intention, to gain wisdom and insight about struggles, challenges or conflicts you may be facing in your life. Skip the introduction and begin with the breathing practice. Using a stone is optional. Hold only one intention at a time as you journey.

Shamanic journeying is a tool that accesses information at the level of the energetic and puts you in communication with Spirit. Processing and accessing information from this higher perspective re-informs your life in an efficient manner. Shamans work to create healing and transformation at the material level by creating change at the level of the energetic.

From a shamanic perspective, your physical body is shaped and informed by the electromagnetic field that surrounds it. This subtle outer body is also known as the light body, the energy body, the luminous body or aura. Your light body informs through thought, feeling, beliefs, archetypal and ancestral patterns, wounds and trauma held within its field. Your life is being created through the filters of this information.

The matter of your physical body is literally shaped through patterns of darkness and light emitted through your luminous energy body. Grief held in your heart appears more dark and dense in your energy body. This darkness is a pattern, or program, sending information into your physical body through your chakras. Chakras are vortexes that connect your luminous body to your physical body with seven major centers located along your spine. Your physical body receives this program of dark, dense grief and, in response creates a myriad of symptoms such as chest pain, muscle tightness, restricted breathing, shortness of breath, weight gain, fatigue, heaviness in the heart or a stooped posture.

To create change, you can work at the arduous level of body and mind with a certain amount of success. Using the example above, unresolved grief could energize a pattern that uses food to numb the heavy, dense feeling. Excessive physical weight is driven by the excessive emotional weight carried, all the while playing out the sacred drama of the saboteur, who creates self-destructive habits, sabotaging your best interests at every success. To lose the weight, you diet, exercise and repeat daily affirmations. With time, and considered effort, pounds drop. How often do you find yourself back where you started? How often does the weight you worked so hard to lose, return? This does not negate the value of diet and exercise, or affirmations, but unless the patterns driving the weight are brought to light, all formidable efforts are spent in vain.

When grief is honored and held in ceremony, it can be released. In the ceremonial letting go, lightness emerges. No longer does the weight of grief inform your life. When the saboteur no longer hides in shadows, undermining you at every turn, it becomes your ally. Its voice can expose hidden fears and agendas, alerting you to what needs attention to deepen your commitment to a course of action or change.

Just as it is easier to alter the downstream course of a river from upstream, so too is it easier to work from a higher perspective to create the life you seek. New patterns and pathways re-inform your life at every level. Struggle and effort drop as you step into the flow of grace. Your heart aligns with a higher calling. This is the life your soul has been longing for.

ALTAR

*"We are not human beings on a spiritual journey.
We are spiritual beings on a human journey."*
PIERRE TEILHARD DE CHARDIN

1. An altar is a sacred space created by placing or arranging objects with a specific intention. It offers focus for prayer, meditation and healing. An altar is a reminder that everything in life is sacred as placing something on an altar elevates it to the level of the sacred. The more you use an altar, the stronger it becomes.

2. Today you will create an altar to honor your Spirit ally. This is one way to cultivate and strengthen the relationship with your ally. An altar need not be elaborate. To create your altar start with a small cloth. You can use a bandana, a large cotton napkin or a personal fabric or textile. Designate a space that is clean and clutter free and lay your altar cloth there. This is where you will place your stone. Your altar will become home for your Spirit ally. If you already have an altar, there is no need to create a new one. You can designate a space on your altar for your Spirit ally. That choice is up to you.

3. Recognize that an altar is a living energetic entity, fed and nourished by your attention and intention. Pay attention to your altar each day to cultivate this relationship. If you forget or miss a day, do not abandon your altar. Simply re-remember, time and again. This is the gift of the sacred. The invitation to return is always available.

4. Lighting a candle on your altar will feed it. Burning incense or sage is another way to feed your altar. Place a small bowl or plate on your altar to feed it with offerings such as grains, sweets, tobacco or chocolate. Fresh flowers will feed your altar. Sitting in prayer and meditation with your altar will energize it.

5. Whatever you place on your altar, do so with intention. If you make an offering, or light your candle, do so with a sense of heartfelt gratitude and appreciation for your Spirit ally. This will begin to deepen the connection with your Spirit ally. The sacred language of Spirit is spoken through prayer, ceremony and ritual. This communication forever deepens on your path.

6. Watch yourself in this process of creating an altar. Do you feel things have to be perfect? Do you think your altar is not enough? Is there a tendency to think you have to fill up your altar space? Notice the way you come to create your altar. How do the patterns that show up here show up in other aspects of your life? How you do anything is how you do everything. Write anything you notice here.

7. Your altar is also a space that can hold any discomfort, questions, feelings or uncertainties that may arise while using this journal. If you notice you are feeling fearful or anxious you can write that on a piece of paper and place it on your altar. In this way you are making an offering of everything you feel and elevating it to the sacred where the potential for transformation and guidance from Spirit is created.

8. You might have a belief that something is sacred only if it is positive or good or some other attribute your mind may apply to what is sacred. As you cultivate a spiritual path you come to see that everything is sacred. You begin to honor and acknowledge the beauty in both the darkness and the light. An altar is one way to help elevate everything to the level of the sacred.

9. List 5 things you are grateful for today.

BODY SCAN

"There is more wisdom in your body
than in your deepest philosophies."
FRIEDRICH NIETZCHE

1. Today you will begin your daily practice by following the *Body Scan*. This guided practice will heighten your awareness to thoughts, feelings and sensations in your own body. Find a comfortable seated position. Follow the guided instructions. You will need about 12 minutes to complete this practice. Notice what stood out or seemed significant for you during this practice. Write that here.

2. Your body orients you to time and space. It lets you know where you are at any given moment. The more you embody your body, the more you become oriented to the present moment, that which is happening now. As you heighten your awareness to thoughts, feelings and sensations, you may begin to notice that much of your attention is scattered away in thought. In thought, your attention is pulled into the future, or drawn into the past. At that moment, the awareness of your body is lost, preoccupied in the stories, dramas and chatter running through your mind.

3. This mind chatter is a very effective coping strategy. At some point in your life this was a brilliant choice to ensure survival. It allowed you to avoid being in your body. To be in your body means you must feel. To avoid feeling, the busyness of mind offers an immediate distraction.

4. There are many reasons to leave your body, including the pain of trauma, abuse, criticism and shame. In the shamanic tradition, this loss of vital energy is called soul loss. As a method to manage feelings that overwhelm or threaten your very existence, a part of yourself retreats from your physical body, escaping into non-ordinary states of reality.

5. The *Body Scan* can fortify your ability to hold sensation in your body that at one time may have felt too threatening. It increases your capacity to stay present to what you feel without relying on patterns of avoidance, distraction and numbing. Increasing the strength of your energy body creates the possibility to recover the vital energy of your soul once lost. For any relationship to thrive, attention is necessary. This includes the relationship with your body and soul.

6. Take a moment to notice your reaction to the *Body Scan*. Was it difficult to slow down or stay present to the guided instructions? Did you find yourself easily distracted; wandering off in thought or plans for your day? Were you critical of the process, making mental comments about the guided instruction, music or voice? Were you anxious, impatient or bored? Did you wish you were somewhere else thinking there were better things you could be doing with your time? Were you able to complete the entire scan? The practice of intention requires a focused awareness in the present moment. Write what you notice here.

7. List 5 things you are grateful for today.

INNER SMILE

*"One of the most responsible things you can do as an adult
is to become more of a child."*

DR. WAYNE DYER

1. As part of your daily practice follow the *Inner Smile*. You will need about 10 minutes to complete this practice. Find a comfortable space to lie on your back. Notice what stood out or seemed significant. Write that here.

2. The *Inner Smile* is an ancient Tao practice. The Taoists were well aware of the healing energy a smile carries. Recall what it feels like to receive a smile, especially unexpectedly. Something inside you lights up. A smile carries with it healing energy. It is this healing energy you will give to yourself in this practice.

3. Once you learn the *Inner Smile*, you can use it anytime, especially during times of stress. With practice, a few minutes of an inner smile can reduce the stress load on your body, allowing you to handle the obstacles of day-to-day life with greater ease.

4. The *Inner Smile* can also be directed to any area of your body in need of healing. This can be an area of pain or recovery, a place that holds past wounds or trauma. As you send your inner smile to these areas within, enhance this practice by placing your hands on your body as well. Imagine sending white light through your hands along with your inner smile for a practice of self-healing. If there is any part of you in need of healing, make this part of a daily practice for yourself.

5. List 5 things you are grateful for today.

INNER GARDEN

"Whoever loves and understands a garden
will find contentment within."
CHINESE PROVERB

1. As part of your daily practice follow the *Inner Garden*. This practice will help you discover and release inner tensions as you create space to cultivate the seeds of your becoming. Find a comfortable seated position. Follow the guided instructions. You will need about 15 minutes for this practice. Write what stood out from your experience here.

2. Metaphorically, manifesting intention is much like gardening. Intention is planted as a seed through thought and feeling. The seed of intention holds within all that is needed for it to manifest, just as the seed of an acorn holds within the great oak. If we live with the faith of an acorn, creation and manifestation become our birthright. Yet life has a way of triggering fear, doubt and worry, the weeds that choke all potential for intention to blossom. Just as you tend to a garden so flowers may grow and bloom, so too you must give care and attention to the inner landscape from which you create your life. The more you clear the metaphorical weeds of doubt, fear, demons and self sabotage, the more you allow the brilliance of Spirit to nourish and feed the seeds of your intention.

3. List 5 things you are grateful for today.

*"Forget not that the Earth
delights to feel your bare feet,
and the winds long to play with your hair."*

KAHIL GIBRAN

SQUARE BREATHING

"The mind commands the body and it obeys.
The mind orders itself and meets resistance."
SAINT AUGUSTINE

1. As part of your daily practice follow the instruction for *Square Breathing*. This is a simple breathing technique that reduces stress and shifts the state of your mental and emotional body. Find a comfortable seated position. You will need approximately 12 minutes. Write what stood out from your experience or note any shifts from this practice.

2. *Square Breathing* uses a diaphragmatic, three part breathing pattern. Take a moment to practice it here before you begin. Inhale by expanding your lower abdomen. Feel it inflate like a balloon. Feel your inhalation rise up from your belly to your ribs. Your inhalation completes at the top of your chest. Your exhalation begins from the top of your chest and slowly lowers back to the belly. Your exhalation completes by pulling your navel in towards your spine. Feel a contraction of your lower abdominal muscles as you completely empty your breath. This instruction is also repeated during the *Square Breathing* practice on track 5.

3. Your thoughts, moods and feelings are reflected in the way you breathe. Imagine the constriction of your breath in the midst of an angry argument compared to the sacred quality of your breath while holding a newborn baby. What is happening in your thoughts and feelings are mirrored in your breath. Square breathing is one way to consciously slow down the rhythm of your breath thereby altering your body's physiological response to thoughts and feelings.

4. Become aware of your breath today. Notice at any given moment how your breath feels. Do you notice restriction, contentment, depth or tightness? Is your breath shallow? Do you hold your breath? How much air do you take in with each breath? Breath is the spark that awakens

your life, infusing your body with Spirit. Watch your breath. Recognize the sacred life force that enters your body with each inhalation. When your body becomes a deeper container for breath, you create within a deeper vessel for Spirit to dwell.

5. List 5 things you are grateful for today.

HEART OF PEACE

"I honor the place in you in which the entire Universe dwells.
I honor the place in you that is of love, truth, of light and of peace.
When you are in that place in you and I am in that place in me, we are one."
NAMASTE PRAYER

1. As part of your daily practice follow *Heart of Peace*. This practice will expand the sense of peace within you and around you. Prepare yourself by taking a comfortable seated position. You will need about 10 minutes to complete this practice. Notice what stood out or seemed significant. Write that here.

2. You see the world around you through your eyes. How you perceive your world is through your heart. If you are holding resentment in your heart, this resentment will be seen in your world through certain circumstances or relationships in your life. If you are holding anger in your heart, this anger will be appear in the world around you. If you are holding beauty in your heart, then your world is perceived through the eyes of beauty. Imagine perceiving your life through a smile in your heart? Do you perceive your life through a critical eye? Notice where this criticism lives in your own heart. Recognize this intimate connection of what you are holding in your heart, and what you perceive through your eyes.

3. List 5 things you are grateful for today.

LETTING GO OF EXPECTATIONS

"We don't have an eternity to realize our dreams,
only the time we are here."
SUSAN L. TAYLOR

1. As part of your daily practice follow *Letting Go of Expectations.* This practice will help release attachment to how your intention unfolds. To prepare for this practice find a comfortable seated position. You will need about 12 minutes to complete this. Follow the guided instructions. Take a moment to reflect on your experience. Notice what stood out or seemed significant. Write what you notice here.

2. The desire to control the circumstances and events in your life is a function of your mind. This practice of intention is a co-creation with Spirit. This dance with Spirit is not one that follows a linear or predictable path. You are asked to fortify your faith and surrender your fear to trust. This leap can feel unsettling since the mind wants to know. The mind wants to be certain. The mind prefers a predictable course to ensure safety and security. The mind is a tool and as such is there to serve. Very often mind has become elevated to master, believing it has dominion over Spirit. To co-create with Spirit, mind must surrender to an infinite Intelligence, a source of wisdom beyond all reason of mind.

3. List 5 things you are grateful for today.

DAY 10   DATE _____

ATTITUDE OF GRATITUDE

"The best and most beautiful things in the world
cannot be seen nor touched but are felt in the heart."
HELEN KELLER

1. As part of your daily practice follow *Attitude of Gratitude*. This practice will awaken a sacred awareness of your body. It offers an opportunity to thank your body for all the service it so willingly provides. Before you begin, find a space where you can lie comfortably on the floor, or as close to the Earth as possible. If you are distracted by any discomfort in your body, try placing a pillow under your knees or beneath your head for support. You will need approximately 12 minutes to complete this practice. Take a moment to reflect on your experience during this practice. What stood out or seemed significant? What, if anything, changed or shifted in your awareness after completing this process? Write what you notice here.

2. Do you know anyone who would work 24 hours a day, 7 days a week, day in, day out, never taking a break and never once receiving a thank you for their tireless efforts? Think of all the jobs your body performs every day. Your heart has not stopped pumping since your time in the womb. Your lungs continually regulate the flow of oxygen essential to your survival. Like an ever-running steam engine, your digestive system converts what you eat into fuel, providing energy to function. The jobs required to sustain your life every day are endless. Treating your body with appreciation helps heal and restore right relationship between you and your body. Holding your body sacred helps bring the sense of sacred to everything in your life.

3. Listen to the inner wisdom of your own body. Ask what it needs to feel nourished and supported. Does it require more rest, more water, more greens, more movement, fresh air?

Listen and wait for a response. What is one thing you can do today to demonstrate this appreciation for your body and honor its needs? Write that here.

4. List 5 things you are grateful for today.

The Guest House

This being human is a guest house.
Every morning a new arrival.

A joy, a depression, a meanness,
some momentary awareness comes
as an unexpected visitor.

Welcome and entertain them all!
Even if they're a crowd of sorrows,
who violently sweep your house
empty of its furniture,
still, treat each guest honorably.
He may be clearing you out
for some new delight.

The dark thought, the shame, the malice,
meet them at the door laughing,
and invite them in.

Be grateful for whoever comes,
because each has been sent
as a guide from beyond.

RUMI

AT HOME

"A house is a home when it shelters the body and comforts the soul."
PHILLIP MOFFITT

1. As part of your daily practice follow *At Home*. This practice will heighten your awareness to the ease in which you are at home in your body. To prepare for this practice find a comfortable seated position. You will need about 12 minutes to complete this practice. Take a moment to reflect on your experience. Notice what stood out, what seemed significant? Notice how this practice influenced or changed anything you noticed in your body. Write your reflections here.

2. Your body is home for Spirit to dwell and as such its architecture is sacred. Through your body, the sanctity of your soul is animated and expressed through voice, movement and action. What kind of home are you creating for Spirit? Does your Spirit dwell in a spacious palace or is Spirit confined to narrow and constricted spaces with little room for breath or expression?

3. As you begin to recognize your body as the sacred temple it is, you will see how the negative self talk and critical thoughts are desecrating your divine home. Imagine entering a sacred place of worship and denigrating its walls with words and images of slander and defamation. This is exactly what you do when you listen to the harsh criticism of your own negative thinking. It is nothing less than slander and defamation of your own sacred temple.

4. List 5 things you are grateful for today.

Purification Practices and Cleansing Rituals

Purification practices have been a part of spiritual traditions throughout the ages. At the heart of these cleansing rituals lies the element of water. When water combines with prayer a cleansing ritual is created that harmonizes body and soul. Ritual cleansing is believed to invoke a state of purity and allow prayers to be more heartfelt.

Although purification practices are ancient in tradition, they are especially relevant today given the demands of our modern day lifestyles. One of the benefits of purification practices is that they

rebalance our energy fields by enhancing the charge of negative ions. Positive and negative ions occur naturally in the atmosphere however modern lifestyles have created an overabundance of positive ions in our environment.

Your energy body is an electromagnetic field that surrounds your physical body much like the atmosphere that surrounds our planet Earth. Cell phones, computers, fluorescent lighting and many of the developments of our modern day world leave us exposed to an abundance of positive ions. Do not confuse positive with something that is good for you. An abundance of positive ions, like the ones we receive from computers and cell phones, drain our system of negative ions creating an imbalance. An imbalance in our electromagnetic field will show up in the body as a whole range of symptoms including fatigue, irritability, depression and/or headaches.

It feels so good to walk in the woods or along the beach since the air in these natural environments, by the ocean, waterfalls, mountains and forests, are highly charged with negative ions and help restore our own systems to complete and natural balance.

A variety of practices are offered here to help integrate daily cleansing rituals into your lifestyle in ways that are manageable and beneficial. Adding sea salt enhances the purification properties when combined with a cleansing ritual. Sea salt provides a deep exfoliation for the skin, the largest organ in your body. A major function of your skin is to eliminate waste. When this organ is clear, the elimination processes of your body are fortified, helping to maintain energetic harmony.

Now, more than ever, it is important to understand the environmental stresses we face and bring conscious awareness to restoring balance for the health of body, mind and soul.

PURIFICATION

"The body is your temple.
Keep it pure and clean for the soul to reside in."
B.K.S. IYENGAR

1. As part of your daily practice follow the *Body Scan*. Note what stood out from your experience today. Write that here.

2. Water and prayer create a cleansing ritual. The simplest way to bring this practice of purification into your day is during your time in the shower. As you stand under the water, thank the water for its cleansing and purification. Ask that any impurities or negativities be removed from your system. It is these dark and dense energies, also called hucha, that get in the way of knowing the lightness of your own Being.

3. I have written a prayer for purification that you can follow for this practice if you like. You do not need to recite it word for word but it offers the essence of a prayer you can use until your own heartfelt prayer arises, for it is the prayer residing in your own heart that has the most power.

4. Using sea salt during your shower is a powerful purification and energy cleansing practice. Start by stepping under the shower to wet your body. As you step out from under the water, scrub your entire body with fine sea salt with the strong intention of clearing anything from your system that no longer serves you. Scrub vigorously while you hold the intention of clearing the energetic patterns that have created the old stories, belief systems and ways of being that you want to release. You can work with a specific and personal intention such as clearing anger or resentment towards someone. Spend a few minutes with this process so that every part of your body feels clear.

5. Follow your sea salt scrub by standing under the shower as you feel the water wash these patterns from your very essence. Thank the waters for their cleansing and purification with your prayers.

6. A more elaborate cleansing ritual is a spiritual bath. When you have time I highly recommend creating a spiritual bath for yourself before you complete this journal. Create a healing sanctuary by filling your bathroom with candlelight. Fill your tub with water as hot as you can tolerate. Add 1 cup of sea salt and 1 cup baking soda for an energetic detox. You can also add flowers or herbs to enhance the healing properties of your bath and re-inform your body with the energetic properties of the plants you are using. Lavender is soothing for the mental and emotional body, rosemary is a strong detoxer, roses enhance healing issues of the heart, marigolds are good general spiritual cleansers. Notice if any herbs or flowers call to you for this process. Blow your prayers of gratitude into any flowers or herbs that you add to your bath, thanking them for their healing. Send your prayers of gratitude, of healing, of cleansing and purification into the waters with good, strong intention.

7. If you are not able to take a full bath, you can apply the same methods above to a footbath and cleansing.

8. The same purification practices can be integrated while washing your hands. Your hands are an extension of your heart. The touch of your hands has the power to soothe and heal. Your hands are powerful transmitters of energy. They can also become areas where energy becomes stuck, especially if you have not been able to let the life force of your own heart flow.

9. Another way to energetically clear your hands is to keep a bowl of sea salt readily available. You can use the sea salt dry. Scoop up some salt with your hands and give them a good, vigorous rub all over. Let the salt fall back into the bowl as you can continue to reuse it. This is an especially good practice if you are a healer, massage therapist or anyone who can potentially pick up energetic disturbances from others through their hands. You will notice an immediate difference in the feel and texture of your skin.

10. Being able to perform purification rituals with water in the natural world is always profound. If you are fortunate enough to live near a river, stream, lake or ocean, walk through the waters as you pray with heartfelt gratitude for cleansing and purification. Spend as much time as you can in this sacred, prayerful communion. Once you leave the waters, walk barefoot along the Earth asking to be re-informed by the beauty of Pachamama, Mother Earth; asked to be

re-informed by her abundance and fertility, asked to be re-informed by her ancient wisdom and healing ways.

11. Working with water in this way will change your relationship to the natural world. You begin to recognize the sacredness of this powerful and life-sustaining element. You begin to open and allow yourself to be informed by water and what it has to teach you. You recognize this element within you, your own fluid nature. Let yourself be informed by the ways of water as you learn to move in flow with your own life.

12. Make a note of how you will incorporate a cleansing or purification ritual into your day.

13. List 5 things you are grateful for today.

Prayer to the Waters for Purification

Dear Pachamama,
I am called to your waters,
for cleansing and purification.
Thank you for washing clean from my system
the energetic impressions of lack and limitation
that have informed and shaped my life.
Thank you for clearing and cleansing
the sorrows and wounds,
the fear and shame
from every cell,
every tissue,
so that I may be re-informed by your beauty Pachamama.

Let these patterns be washed clean
so that I may be re-informed by your fertility and abundance.
Let these patterns that no longer serve,
be washed clean from my essence
so that I may be re-informed
by your ways of mystery and magic,
re-informed by your wisdom.

~HEYA OM~

ACTION STEP

"Heaven never helps the man who will not act."
SOPHOCLES

1. As part of your daily practice follow the *Inner Smile*. Write what stood out from your experience here.

2. Today you will create an action step, boldly taking your life in the direction of your intention. An action step is not another thing to put on your "to do" list becoming a chore or obligation in your day. An action step arises from a passion that fuels your movement in the direction of your desires.

3. As you bring to mind your intention, note one thing you could do today that would support you in creating this intention in your life. Is there some action you could take, a phone call you could make, some information you need to gather, a contact you have been meaning to reach out to? An action step could also be more about being, less about doing. Would it serve you to spend time in meditation, sit quietly, take a walk in the woods or perhaps take a nap?

4. Let your action step be achievable TODAY so create something realistic and manageable for yourself given the time and logistics of your day. Rather than creating a "to do" list, notice what it would be like if your action arose from a "to feel" list. Write your action step here.

5. List 5 things you are grateful for today.

6. If you were not able to complete your action step today notice what got in the way? What stopped you? Write that here.

CONVERSATION WITH SPIRIT

"The day, water, sun, moon, night;
I do not have to purchase these things with money."
PLAUTIS

1. As part of your daily practice follow the *Inner Garden.* Notice what stood out or seemed significant for you. Write that here.

2. We are well versed in the language of mind as it communicates to us through thought. Most of what we speak about relates to what we are thinking. Spirit speaks to us through our soul. The language of soul is rich in imagery and symbols. Poetry and music arise from soul. Your dreams are an example of communication in this realm. You may feel baffled when it comes to understanding the poetic language of your soul. Understanding this language of soul begins by listening.

3. To start a conversation with your Spirit ally, find a quiet place to sit for a moment. Place your stone in your left hand. Your left side is your dominant receptive channel. Clear your mind with a few deep breaths.

4. Always come to a conversation with Spirit starting with thank you. Offer a prayer of gratitude. Thank the stone for serving and informing you. Thank your Spirit ally for making them known to you.

5. Once you have said a prayer of thanks, you can begin a conversation with your Spirit ally by asking their name. Ask how they would like to be called. Open your internal channels of listening to receive. Let this information arise. Relax and wait for a response. Do not rush or force anything. Develop your capacity to listen, to sit and be still.

6. Once you have received a name do not reveal this to anyone. Do not write it down here. It is for you only. Holding the name will hold its power. You can use the name to call forth and connect with your Spirit ally without using the stone. Once you tell someone the name you begin to dissipate the power of this connection. This one person may tell someone and they tell someone else and in this way an energetic leak is created. The connection loses its potency. So do not reveal the name to anyone.

7. Some other questions that are good to begin a conversation with your Spirit ally are:

    *   Do you have a message for me?

    *   What gifts do you bring?

    *   What have you come to teach me or show me?

    *   What do you need from me?

8. This last one is especially important to ask. The relationship you cultivate with Spirit is reciprocal in nature thereby creating balance and harmony, or what shamans call ayni. If one partner in a relationship is the one making all the effort while the other sits idly by, that relationship is out of balance. This is also true in your relationship with Spirit.

9. Being in conversation with Spirit opens your ability to listen. Listening is an alert, engaged state of receptivity. Many of us have learned to shut down our capacity to listen as a way to avoid what we did not want to hear. If you find you are unable to receive any information from your stone, begin to pay attention to your ability to listen. This will serve you in all your relationships.

10. As mentioned earlier, another way to be in communication with your ally is through dreams. Place your stone under your pillow and ask for guidance while you sleep. This is another method to source information from.

11. As you become more comfortable being in conversation with your ally, listening and receiving information, you can begin to ask advice or seek guidance on questions regarding your life.

12. It is helpful to know how to frame a question to receive the information you seek. Avoid asking questions with a yes or no answer. If you have a question about a relationship, rather than ask, "Should I end this relationship?" ask, "Show me what I need to see in my relationship." Ask questions specific to your intention:

- What is my purpose?

- What does my soul long to express?

- What limiting beliefs keep me from moving ahead?

- What structure can I create to support my intention?

- What support does my soul need from me?

13. Over time, as you cultivate this relationship, you will discover a rich source of wisdom you can rely on. Trust the impressions you receive, even if they don't make sense right away or if you think something can't possibly be right. Walking a path with Spirit teaches you to trust your own perceptions, trust your own inner voice, trust your own feelings and trust your direct experience. That can be challenging if you have become accustomed to seek the approval of others for validation of your own truth.

14. List 5 things you are grateful for today.

Prayer

Prayer is your intimate conversation with the Divine, the language that calls forth Spirit, an offering that expresses itself through the poetry of your heart. Prayer honors the intelligence of Spirit, allowing the power of Spirit to shine ever more brightly.

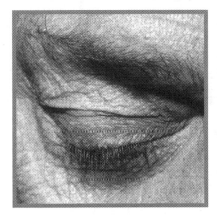

How did you learn to pray? Was it through a mechanical recitation of words over which you had little understanding? Was it through rote memorization and repetition? Were you taught to listen to the quiet voice within? Were the feelings and sensitivities of your own heart held in value? Did prayer arise from dogma or intellect? Could you hear your tender heart whisper its longings? Was God separate from you, kept at a distance? Was the power of God something to be feared?

Was prayer something you turned to in need or crisis? Did prayer arise in sheer desperation when all other hope seemed lost? Did you come to prayer like a beggar, pleading for mercy, wondering why you received only crumbs? Are your prayers pretentious directions to Spirit on how to heal, correct or resolve a situation?

A shaman stops to pray when climbing a mountain; not to ask to make it to the top, but rather to give thanks for the blessing of making it as far as they have already come. Imagine prayer arising from this place. What if your prayer was an expression of the appreciation and gratitude for the blessings that already exist in such abundance? How could prayer in this way transform your relationship to Spirit and your life?

In the shamanic tradition of the Andes, prayers are blown into qintus. A qintu is made with three cocoa leaves, native to that part of the world and held as sacred. A prayer is then transferred to the qintu through the breath. The breath is the energetic conduit on which the prayer travels. The qintu is then offered to the Earth, returned to the elements.

This way of praying creates an energetic alignment that restores right relationship, or what shamans call ayni, with our place in the world. Ayni is a place of being in balance and harmony within your own heart and from that place within, balance and harmony is reflected in the world around you.

How often are our prayers laden with the results we expect, the desire for more comfort, abundance, ease or happiness, wanting even more spiritual knowledge? Praying in this way obstructs the channels of communication with Spirit, blocking the ability for Spirit to work through our life. Human nature does not see the mystical matrix, the mystery behind the ways of Spirit. We want our prayers to free us from suffering. We long to leap to the end of our soul's process of learning, to a place that offers comfort and ease. Yet our soul yearns to experience every facet of human experience while it is here, in human form. Sometimes this includes a path of discomfort to motivate fundamental change on a path of liberation.

The way we pray matters. For a prayer arising from soul, offered with heartfelt intention, is always heard and held in the most exquisite grace.

EARTH PRAYERS

"Nature does not hurry, yet everything is accomplished."
LAO TZU

1. As part of your daily practice follow *Square Breathing*. Notice what stood out or seemed significant for you. Write that here.

2. Mother Earth has provided everything in your life; the food you eat, the air you breathe, the clothes you wear, the home you live in. She is the Divine Mother manifest in its most majestic form. We can never say thank you to her enough.

3. Today your intention is to offer your prayers to Mother Earth throughout your day. Using your breath, and an offering from nature, your prayers will begin to restore your alignment with Nature and all things of the Universe. This readjustment of righting your relationship to yourself and your place in the world is known by shamans as ayni. Ayni is a place that resides in your heart. Words do not describe ayni as words are of the mind and ayni resides beyond. Yet being in ayni comes with a knowing. There is a deep ease of being at home, at one with everything. Duality does not exist here. There is no sense of right, wrong, good, bad. Offering your prayers in this way begins to bring you into ayni, the longing of your heart to return home.

4. In different traditions, tobacco, flowers or cocoa leaves are used to hold prayers. Today you will find something in your own kitchen or native surroundings that will work for you. Grains like rice or dried beans, fresh or dried herbs, flower petals, small leaves, organic sugar, seeds, nuts or raisins are just some of the things you could use as prayer offerings. See what causes a knowing in your heart. Trust that you already have what you need to make your prayer offerings.

5. Once you know what you are going to use, place your offering items in a small bag you can carry with you for your day. When you blow your prayers into your offering you will need a good pinch or small handful of whatever you are using. If using leaves or flower petals, you can create a qintu by using three at a time to hold your prayer offering.

6. Every good prayer begins with a thank you. As you offer your prayers, hold a sense of gratitude, love and appreciation for Pachamama, Mother Earth. Let your prayer be one of thanks for the glory of the day, thanks for the beauty that Pachamama offers so abundantly, thanks for the warmth of the sun on your face, the blessings in your life, whatever arises from your feeling of thank you. Allow your prayer to be an authentic expression of the calling of your heart. When poetry arises you know you have found the sacred song of your own soul.

7. Your prayers can be said silently or out loud, and spoken, as well as blown, into your prayer offering. Your breath is the energetic conduit that transfers your prayer to your offering so the whispers of your heart may be carried in the winds to commune with the Infinite.

8. Release your prayer offerings back to the Earth. You can scatter them over the grass, place them at the base of a tree, send them into the wind or release them to the waters. Wherever you are today offer your prayers in this way. Your prayers are part of your intimate conversation with Spirit so start with a thank you and allow the rest of your prayer to emerge from the longing of your heart. As you begin to walk through your world in this way the wisdom of your heart guides you and you feel your connectedness to all things.

9. As you pass the beauty of a flower, offer your prayers to this flower for sharing her beauty with you. Notice how sweetly the moss sits at the bottom of the tree and say thank you for touching me with your sweetness. Notice the character of the natural world. Asked to be re-informed by the patience of the trees, the strength of the grasses, the fertility of the waters, the wisdom living in every rock and stone. Ask to feel the heartbeat of Pachamama beat in rhythm with your own. Open your senses today to the miraculous wonders that exist all around you. Offer your thanks for the beauty of this world we live in.

10. Along with prayers of gratitude to Pachamama, you can offer your prayers to ask for her help and guidance with current obstacles, struggles or limitations in your life. Thank her for taking these from you so that you may be re-informed by her wisdom, her beauty and her abundance.

11. List 5 things you are grateful for today.

CELEBRATION

*"Certain things catch your eye but pursue only
those things that capture your heart."*
NATIVE AMERICAN SAYING

1. As part of your daily practice follow *Heart of Peace.* Notice what stood out for you or seemed significant. Write that here.

2. Take a moment to reflect on your journey so far. Look back on this journal from the beginning. Read your journal entries, your reflections, awareness and insight. Feel the investment of your time and energy as you look through these pages.

3. Celebrate your commitment and dedication to this process so far. Honor and acknowledge yourself in a heartfelt way. Find a way to bring a sense of celebration to your day today. Notice what a sense of celebration feels like for you. Your celebration can be simple, such as lighting a candle on your altar to honor your efforts. Create a prayer for yourself. Buy fresh flowers to reflect your own beauty. Have a special dinner.

4. Tell at least one person today about your personal journey you have committed to and how you have been doing. Ask yourself, what can I do to honor myself today? What is good for me? Write your idea for celebration here.

5. Notice if your tendency is to find fault with what you have done up to now feeling there is no reason to celebrate. Are you focusing on all the things you have not done, places you think you may have fallen short? Is it difficult for you to acknowledge your efforts to others? Do you think this idea of celebrating makes no sense? If you are diminishing yourself here, you are diminishing yourself in other aspects of your life. Notice where else any self-sabotaging patterns show up in your life. Write what you notice here.

6. List 5 things you are grateful for today.

DEAR DIARY

"Return to the inner Spirit,
which we have abandoned while looking elsewhere for happiness."
WILLARU HUAYTA, QUECHUA NATION, PERU

1. As part of your daily practice follow *Letting Go of Expectations*. Notice what stood out or seemed significant. Write that here.

2. Thoughts are invisible. Writing them on paper makes them seen moving energy from the invisible realms to the visible. Through writing, you literally create magic, making seen that which previously was not.

3. Use the following page to write a diary entry about what a day of living in your intention is like. Keep your language in the present tense so it feels like what you are writing is happening now. Write your diary entry from the place of feeling your intention, generating your story from imagining the passion and enthusiasm that comes with living your intention.

4. Lift off your mental lid and think big. Keep your pen moving until you fill the entire page. Try not to think too much about what you are writing as you allow your pen to flow from the feelings generated by your imagination. You may surprise yourself at what comes up.

5. Once you are done, read your diary entry out loud. Notice what feelings arise as you read your story. Write what you notice here.

6. List 5 things you are grateful for today.

Dear Diary,

FACING FEAR

"Fear is a natural reaction to moving closer to the truth."
PEMA CHODRON

1. As part of your daily practice follow *Attitude of Gratitude*. Notice what stood out or seemed significant. Write that here.

2. Fear constricts your energy, keeps you stuck, safe and limited. You literally become frozen. What are you afraid of doing in your life right now? Is there someone you are withholding communication from because you are afraid they will be angry? Is there an idea you are afraid to put forth because it might be rejected? Is there a bill you are afraid to open because you fear there won't be enough money to pay for it? Are you putting off ending a relationship because you are afraid of being alone? Are you afraid to speak up for fear of humiliation? Is it difficult to relax because you are afraid to feel?

3. List 5 fears, big and small, you are currently facing in your life.

4. Choose one fear you would like to work with. It need not be the biggest one. Today you will come to know your fear more intimately by creating a dialogue. You will listen and respect your fear to understand more deeply what its needs are, what its message is for you and how your fear can become your ally. The fear of facing your fear is its hook. This dialogue creates on opening, a shift in relationship to your fear, and it is there transformation happens.

5. State clearly what your fear is here. Be specific. Use as much detail as possible regarding what you are afraid of, how it impacts your life, the consequences of the fear on your future, how your fear effects others.

6. Nothing you feel, including your fear, is there by accident. There is wisdom held within your fear. To begin your dialogue, create time and space for you to be quiet, sit still and reflect. Do not rush this process or force anything to happen. You are seeking the wisdom held within your fear by creating a dialogue. Stay open and present to your experience. Do not think about your answers. Do not second-guess what arises. Write the first response to your question. Trust what emerges. Be present to your fear and open your capacity to listen. Respect the wisdom held within your fear. Other questions may arise during this process. If so include them, along with the answers you receive. Trust the process. Trust your impressions. Trust the voice of your own fear. A color, shape or image may arise in response to your question. You may receive no answer. That is your experience. Make note of it, whatever it is. Before you begin, close your eyes to feel, sense and connect with your fear more deeply. Become aware of it in your body. As you are ready, ask the following questions to your fear.

7. Where do you live in my body?

8. How long have you been there?

9. Where did you come from?

10. What lesson can I learn from you?

11. What have you come to teach me?

12. What do you need from me to feel safe?

13. What limiting beliefs do I need to shed to support you?

14. What action can I take to support meeting your needs?

15. Can I take this action today? If not, note when you will be able to follow through with this action.

16. If you were not able to follow through with your action today, what stopped you? What got in the way? Write your experience here.

17. As you unearth parts of yourself that have been hidden in shadow, feelings, anxieties or memories may also come to light. This sacred discomfort arises as you move past limitations into new and sometimes uncomfortable territory. Tomorrow offers instruction in an energetic clearing practice that can assist in moving discomfort through your system. Use purification practices from Day 12 for clearing. Offer your discomfort in prayer. Write what you notice on paper and place it on your altar. Place a symbolic representation of what you feel on your

altar as you light a candle to honor and hold sacred your experience. The breath practices on *Square Breathing* or *Inner Smile* can also help shift energy. Recognize the tools you are building for self care and awareness as you integrate them into your life.

18. List 5 things you are grateful for today including your fear and the wisdom gained.

Parable of the Farmer and the Wheat

Long, long ago, when God still lived on Earth, there was a farmer. One day the farmer came to God and said, "You may be God, and you may have created the world, but one thing is certain, you are not a farmer. You don't even know the first thing about farming. You have something to learn."

God said, "What's your advice?"

The farmer said, "Give me one year and let things be according to me and see what happens. There will be no poverty left!"

God was willing and one year was given to the farmer. Naturally, the farmer asked for the best; no thunder, no strong winds, no dangers for the crops. Everything was comfortable and cozy and the farmer was very happy. The wheat was growing so high! When he wanted sun, there was

sun. When he wanted rain, there was rain, and as much as he wanted. This year everything was right according to the farmer.

When it came time to harvest the crops the farmer was surprised to find no wheat inside. He asked God, "What happened? What went wrong?"

God said, "Because there was no challenge, because there was no conflict, no friction, because you avoided all that was bad, the wheat remained impotent. A little struggle is a must. Storms are needed, thunder, lightening is needed. They shake up the soul inside the wheat."

EMOTIONAL FREEDOM

*"Emotion always has its roots in the unconscious
and manifests itself in the body."*
IRENE CLAREMONT DE CASTILLEJO

1. As part of your daily practice follow *At Home*. Notice what stood out or seemed significant. Write that here.

2. Emotional freedom techniques are a powerful tool to move energy that is stuck or painful through your mental, emotional and physical body. Use this process when you experience pain, distress or discomfort, whenever it arises. It is worth taking a few moments to learn the technique since it is easy to master and highly effective.

3. Take a moment to reflect on thoughts, feelings, behaviors or habits that are getting in the way of creating what you want in your life. Do you tell yourself you're not good enough? Are you afraid to take a risk or fail? Do you procrastinate? Do you doubt yourself? Do you have a hard time speaking up for yourself or saying no? Are you afraid of what other people think of you? Do you smoke, overeat or drink to excess? The intention here is not to beat yourself up but rather become clear about what patterns are causing you distress so you can begin to create a change. You can also use this technique to help clear pain from your physical body. You may want to work with your fear from the previous day's practice. Make your list here.

4. From your list, decide what you want to work with. Grade the distress this issue is causing by giving it a number. Zero means this issue is creating no pain or distress, 10 is the worst level of pain and distress. It is always important to start this technique with a number so you can determine if you are lowering the level of intensity. Make a mental note of the number.

5. You will now include your self limiting pattern in the following statement: Even though I

_____ ,

I still love and accept myself unconditionally.

6. While you repeat the statement above out loud, you will tap continuously along the outside of your hand, above your wrist and below your pinky finger (also known as the karate chop position, see below). Use the fingertips of your dominant hand (usually index and middle). Continue for about 10 - 15 seconds. Continue to repeat your statement while you tap along the points listed below.

7. The more specific you can make the statement about what you are looking to clear, the more effective the technique is. If you are feeling angry you could say, "Even though I am angry at so and so for criticizing me in front of my boss yesterday, I still love and accept myself unconditionally." Or "Even though I am so ashamed of myself for eating a whole container of ice cream, I still love and accept myself unconditionally." Or "Even though I am so afraid of this pain in my back that won't go away I still love and accept myself unconditionally."

8. The following points are associated with energy meridians in the body and tapping is the method that assists the flow of energy through these channels, helping to clear blockages from your system. Focus on the problem or issue you are looking to clear from your system while you tap the points in the following order.

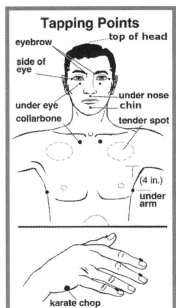

- eyebrow

- side of eye

- under eye

- under nose

- chin

- collar bone/sternum (use the palm of your hand here)

- under arm about 2" below armpit (use the palm of your hand here)

- top of head

9. Continue repeating the cycles of tapping, starting with the karate chop position and ending at the top of the head, until you feel the intensity level of your distress has dropped to a number 2 or 3. This will require a number of cycles, especially if patterns are old or chronic.

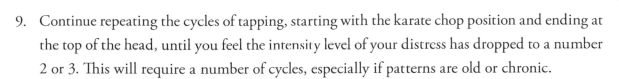

10. Once you feel the intensity level has lowered to a 2 or 3, begin rubbing your hand over the center of your chest in a clockwise direction as you repeat the following statement: *"God is love and so am I."* Substitute God with whatever name you feel comfortable with that conveys an essence of unconditional love, such as Spirit, Nature, the Universe, Existence, Light, the Stars, the Heavens. Continue until you feel the intensity drop to a 1 or Zero.

11. With a little practice, this technique is easy to master and is a very effective tool for clearing your system of pain or intense emotion. Use it if you feel angry with someone to lower the intensity of the feeling. Use it if you are emotionally or mentally overwhelmed. Use it if you are experiencing pain anywhere in your body. Use it anytime you feel agitation, physically, mentally or emotionally.

12. List 5 things you are grateful for today.

JUST SAY YES

"Positive use of emotions means directing our love, directing our emotion toward creative use by becoming a real lover, a lover of humanity."
SWAMI RAMA

1. As part of your daily practice follow the *Body Scan*. Notice what stood out or seemed significant for your. Write that here.

2. Most of us have become conditioned to expect and receive **NO** in response to our thoughts, feelings, ideas and needs, a pattern established early in childhood. With eyes closed repeat the word **NO** to yourself for a minute. This can be done silently or out loud. Feel the essence of **NO** in your body. What do you notice as you tell yourself **NO**? What does **NO** feel like in your body? Write what you notice here.

3. Now with eyes closed repeat the word *YES* to yourself, either silently or out loud for one minute. What does *YES* feel like in your body? Tune into any subtle differences you notice in your body to the word *YES* and the word **NO**. Write what you notice here.

4. For the rest of the day today your practice is **YES**. Both silently and out loud, repeat the word **YES** as often as you remember. This is especially helpful during times of stress, or when there is an aversion to your reality in the moment. **YES** helps you embrace what is happening, gives space and permission to your thoughts and feelings rather than trying to use your energy to suppress them. The subconscious mind receives **YES** as a positive, affirmative statement that reduces stress and strengthens your immune response. **YES** enhances your energy rather than depletes it.

5. Try to start every situation today with **YES.** Notice if **NO** has become a habit. Is **NO** your default program? Is your reaction to a person, thought or new idea automatically **NO**? If you must say **NO** to a person or situation, let it be a result of a conscious choice rather than an automatic reaction. When **NO** is a habitual response, it automatically creates a wall, or barrier. Begin to become aware of the shut down patterns that happen in your body with a fundamental response of **NO**. **NO** does not allow you to receive, whether it is a connection in relationship, a compliment from another or an opportunity from the universe. Notice how much of your life is informed from a place of **NO**, including the essence of your own existence or your relationship with Spirit. Reflect on your awareness here.

6. Another mantra, or sacred sound, that enhances the strength of your energy body is **THANK YOU**. Repeating **THANK YOU**, either silently or out loud, immediately lowers your stress response, especially in response to situations, people, circumstances and feelings you are not grateful for. Start with small things, like sitting in traffic. A silent thank you, offered repeatedly, shifts your experience of sitting in traffic. Instead of feeling irritated, you may come to appreciate the chance to slow down, or recognize the opportunity to cultivate patience. You can extend this practice to situations and feelings that are extremely difficult. Saying thank you under duress may seem simple, but the practice of thank you is not an easy one. Cultivating and integrating gratitude into your body and life is a practice that develops along your spiritual path. Start simple. Remember, it is called practice, not perfection.

7. List 5 things you are grateful for today. Include something challenging. State what makes you grateful for this in your life.

DEAR FEAR

*"When I dare to be powerful,
to use my strength in the service of my vision,
then it becomes less and less important whether I am afraid."*
AUDRE LORDE

1. As part of your daily practice follow the *Inner Smile*. Notice what stood out for you or what seemed significant. Write that here.

2. Your fear is completely dedicated to keeping you safe from what it imagines might be harmful to you. Fear is much like an overprotective mother. It believes it is acting in your best interest, keeping you safe from harm, but in truth, it is limiting your growth and development.

3. Today you will write a heartfelt letter of thanks to your fear. Use your reflections from Day 18 on *Facing Fear*. Let your fear know how much you appreciate all the concern it has shown you. Thank your fear for the security and protection it has so tirelessly provided. Thank your fear for endlessly worrying about your safety, keeping you safe from harm. Let your fear know you understand its concerns and appreciate its loyalty. Let your fear know how much you respect its power. Let your fear know you are ready to release the limitations that your fear has imposed on your body, mind and soul. Let your fear know you are ready to be re-informed by the power and wisdom your fear holds. Let your fear know you are ready to listen to its needs and find support. Thank your fear for expressing its light in your life. Thank your fear for the opportunity to evolve on your path.

4. As you write your letter, let your pen flow from the heartfelt gratitude for your fear. You do not need to include every statement from above in your letter. They are offered as points of reflection and guidance. The most powerful letter is written from the truth of your own heart. Write your letter to fear with gratitude on the following page.

5. List 5 things you are grateful for today.

Dear Fear,

LIMPIAS

"Keep your sense of proportion by regularly,
preferably daily, visiting the natural world."
CATLIN MATTHEWS

1. As part of your daily practice follow the *Inner Garden*. Notice what stood out or seemed significant for you. Write that here.

2. Limpias are a cleansing ritual, often using plants, for harmonizing your energy body. This ritual can be performed for purification and for deepening your connection to Nature, especially if you live in an environment where being out in the natural world is not so easy.

3. Gather herbs from your garden or grocer. Make sure the leaves are still on their stem. As you collect these plants for your limpia maintain an attitude of appreciation in your heart for these natural elements that offer themself to you.

4. Use any herbs or native plants that call to you. Trust the wisdom of your own intuitive guidance. Rosemary is a powerful herb for cleansing since the structure of its DNA has not changed over time, attesting to its strength and fortitude. If you live in parts of the country where evergreens or pine are plentiful, these are excellent plants for limpias. Fresh eucalyptus is another. Maybe you like the smell of basil or peppermint. You can also use flowers. Maybe you are drawn to certain colors. Trust your instincts. Know that you have the wisdom within to know what will serve you. Avoid second-guessing your choices and decisions.

5. Once you have gathered your herbs, plants and/or flowers, you will have a small bundle or bouquet. Grab hold at the bottom and begin using this bouquet to brush yourself from head to toe. Hold the intention of clearing any heavy, dense energy, or hucha, from your system.

Also tap your bundle over your heart, belly and third eye (at the center of your forehead), to clear these major energetic centers. Tapping stimulates energetic and lymphatic flow.

6. Breathe deeply during this process. Let the aromas cleanse as well. You can also sing or chant during this cleansing. If you like, dip your plant bundle in floral water or water scented with essential oils while you perform your limpia using the plants, water and aroma for cleansing.

7. Let your intuitive wisdom guide you through this cleansing. You may move over parts of your body slowly, you may move over others with more vigor. You may spend more time over certain areas of your body or repeatedly stroke or tap in one place. Trust that you know what you need.

8. As with any purification practice, bring prayer to the practice of your limpia. Offer thanks to the plants for taking any hucha, dark, dense energy, from you. Thank Pachamama, Mother Earth, for her healing ways. Ask that any negativities or impurities, be cleansed from your system. You can ask for clearing of a specific emotion, wound or trauma. Clear the pattern of fear you have been working with. Spend some time with this, taking care to work your entire body.

9. Once you are done, offer your bouquet back to the Earth and allow Pachamama to transmute these energies that have been extracted through your plant bundle.

10. Performing limpias in nature is always profound. The next time you are walking in the woods look for pine or evergreen branches. Tap and stroke yourself in heartfelt prayer for healing and cleansing.

11. It is also beautiful to receive a limpia from someone. If there is someone in your life you can share this with, take turns giving and receiving a limpia. Notice how your heartfelt connection deepens through this practice.

12. Not only do these practices cleanse, they also create an opportunity to be in communication with Nature. You align yourself with the natural world, thereby coming into a deeper alignment and order within yourself. You begin to allow Nature to heal you, to inform you, to show you the way.

13. List 5 things you are grateful for today.

MOTHER EARTH DAY

"My profession is to always find God in nature."
HENRY DAVID THOREAU

1. As part of your daily practice follow *Square Breathing*. Notice what stood out or seemed significant for you. Write that here.

2. In the shamanic tradition, Mother Earth, or Pachamama as she is called, is considered our Spiritual Mother, the one who holds the wisdom of the Divine Feminine. Through her infinite benevolence and great compassion she provides everything we need in our life; the food we eat, the air we breathe, the water we drink, the materials that create our clothes, our homes, the medicines for healing. Everything in life arises from the creativity, the fertility, the wisdom, the abundance, the unconditional love of our Spiritual Mother, Pachamama.

3. As you come to know the living, breathing, dynamic, life-giving planet that you live on in this way, you naturally want to show her your love and appreciation, just as you might for the mother who gave birth to you. The ways to show love and appreciation for beloved Pachamama are endless. Today is your Mother Earth Day, an opportunity to consciously express your gratitude for all she has provided for you.

4. Walk on the grass barefoot. Hug or sit with a tree. Breathe fresh air. Tend to a garden. Plant flowers or seeds. Pick up trash. Have you bent to the ground and kissed her in deep and heartfelt appreciation? Watch your own reaction to hugging a tree or kissing the Earth. Acts of love to Mother Earth may feel mechanical rather than heartfelt at first. As your own heart opens to the benevolent abundance that our Earth Mother provides, you will deepen this relationship. These acts will naturally flow from your heart in deep appreciation.

5. Be mindful today of how you use the resources of our planet. Pay attention to the amount of electricity, water and gasoline you use. Are there ways you can reduce your consumption by shutting off lights, turning off water, walking instead of driving? How can you reduce the amount of waste you produce today?

6. These conscious acts of appreciation begin to create a relationship with Pachamama. Space opens within and you cultivate the capacity to listen. Through listening you begin to become re-informed by the ancient wisdom held within her belly. Instead of following the well-worn path of lack and limitation, you begin to follow the heartbeat of Earth Mother, a heartbeat that has nourished and sustained you throughout your life. In this way you come to know your true nature, one that is reflected in the beauty of the Earth, the abundance of the Earth and the sustenance of the Earth. You come to know yourself as a son or daughter of the Earth, a caretaker of the Earth. Write your act of love and appreciation for Mother Earth here.

7. List 5 things you are grateful for today. Include Pachamama.

What lies behind us and what lies before us are tiny matters compared to what lies within us."

RAPLPH WALDO EMERSON

NEW PATHWAYS

"As a single footstep will not make a path on the Earth,
so a single thought will not make a pathway in the mind.
To make a deep physical path, we walk again and again.
To make a deep mental path, we must think over and over
the kind of thoughts we wish to dominate our lives."

HENRY DAVID THOREAU

1. As part of your daily practice follow *Heart of Peace*. Notice what stood out or seemed significant. Write that here.

2. Notice how much of your life has become habit. Where do you feel you are in a rut? Do you take the same route to work everyday? Do you sit in the same spot to watch TV, eat dinner or work on your laptop? Do you eat the same thing for breakfast or lunch, day in and day out? Have you been having the same conversation with someone for years? Watch yourself today as you discover the habits and ruts of well-worn paths and activities.

3. Repeating the same patterns over and over not only create ruts in your day, they create ruts in your mind; well worn grooves that limit your ability to see anything in a new way. Today you will create a new path for yourself. Notice what happens when you change something in a monotonous routine. Change creates an opportunity to see something in a new way. Not only do you create new pathways in your life, you create new pathways in your mind. Neural pathways and connections in your brain are created that were never there before as you break free from habitual patterns and routines. Try turning yourself upside down to get a new perspective! Notice where you can create a change in your daily routine today and open to the possibilities that change offers. Write that here.

4. If you were not able to create a change today, notice what happened. What got in the way? What patterns arise in response to change; resistance, anxiety? If change is difficult for you, you may want to place this on your altar. Write what you notice here.

5. List 5 things you are grateful for today.

DATE _____

DECLUTTER

"To put the world in order, we must first put the nation in order;
to put the nation in order, we must first put the family in order;
to put the family in order, we must cultivate our personal life;
and to cultivate our personal life, we must first set our hearts right."
CONFUCIOUS

1. As part of your daily practice follow *Letting Go of Expectations.* Notice what stood out or seemed significant for you. Write that here.

2. Clutter in your outer world reflects clutter in your inner world. What space in your life needs clearing up? This does not mean you have to tackle the garage or clear out the basement. Find a drawer, a medicine chest, a shelf, a stack of papers that needs to be put in order. Clear out things that you no longer need or no longer serve you. Find a space that you can manage to clear within your day TODAY. Do this with the intention of creating space for your intention in your life. Write what space you will clear here.

3. If you were not able to complete this today notice what got in the way? What stopped you? Note that here.

4. List 5 things you are grateful for today.

GIVEAWAY

"It is not what we take up,
but what we give up, that makes us rich."
HENRY WARD BEECHER

1. As part of your daily practice follow *Attitude of Gratitude*. Notice what stood out or seemed significant. Write that here.

2. The Native American tradition of the Giveaway is an opportunity to give away what is treasured most. Traditionally, what is most valuable is saved to give away, with the understanding that once something is given, all attachments to that gift are broken. A gift is given with nothing expected in return. How often is your motive to give driven by the interests of your own ego, whether you give a gift, a compliment, or even the words I love you? What are we ultimately looking to get whenever we give?

3. Today your focus will be on others. What gift can you give to another that will stretch your heart open? Your Giveaway may be a material gift. Maybe you have something in your personal possession that you know someone else would treasure. Giving away clothes you no longer wear is not in the spirit of the Giveaway.

4. Your Giveaway does not need to be in material form. Your most treasured possession is your heart, your most valuable resource, your time. Is there someone in your life who would benefit from the gift of your company? Is there a neighbor or friend you can reach out to and offer your service in some way? Where can you bring joy by reaching out with a random act of kindness? Have you let someone know how much you appreciate him or her in your life? Is there someone you are holding bitterness, anger or resentment towards? Are you able to give that away to say, "I am sorry" or "Please forgive me" to right a relationship? Can you comfort someone with the words "I love you" and not expect to hear the words spoken in return? Write your Giveaway here.

5. Reflect on the experience of your Giveaway. If you were not able to follow through with the Giveaway today, what got in the way? What stopped you? Write that here.

6. List 5 things you are grateful for today including the experience of your Giveaway.

CLEANSING RITUAL

"Study nature, love nature, stay close to nature.
It will never fail you."
FRANK LLOYD WRIGHT

1. As part of your daily practice follow *At Home.* Notice what stood out or seemed significant. Write that here.

2. Perform a cleansing ritual or purification practice today if they are not part of your daily practice. Review *Limpias* from Day 22 or *Purification Practices* from Day 12. Write your cleansing ritual here.

3. List 5 things you are grateful for today.

ACTION STEP

"Take the first step in faith.
You don't have to see the whole staircase, just take the first step."
DR. MARTIN LUTHER KING, JR.

1. As part of your daily practice follow the *Body Scan*. Notice what stood out or seemed significant. Write that here.

2. Today you will create an action step, boldly taking your life in the direction of your intention. An action step is not another thing to put on your "to do" list thereby creating a chore or obligation in your life. An action step arises from a passion that fuels your movement in the direction of your desires.

3. As you bring to mind your intention, note one thing you could do today that would support you in creating this intention in your life. Is there some action you could take, a phone call you could make, some information you may need to gather or a contact you have been meaning to reach out to? An action step for you may be more about being, less about doing. Would it serve you to spend time in meditation, sit quietly, take a walk in the woods or perhaps take a nap?

4. Let your action step be achievable TODAY so create something realistic and manageable for yourself given the time and logistics of your day. Rather than creating a "to do" list notice what it would be like if your action arose from a "to feel" list.

5. Write your action step here.

6. List 5 things you are grateful for today including taking action.

7. If you were not able to complete your action step today notice what got in the way? What stopped you? Write that here.

STORY TIME

"Not I, nor anyone else, can travel that road for you.
You must travel it for yourself."
WALT WHITMAN

1. As part of your daily practice follow the *Inner Smile*. Notice what stood out for you or seemed significant. Write what you notice here.

2. Your life is shaped by the stories you hold, the stories of your past, your stories of heartbreak, your untold stories, your stories of tragedy, shame, or humiliation, your stories of unspeakable grief and sorrows. Maybe your stories never have a happy ending. Maybe your stories run with themes of loneliness, despair, betrayal or hardship. Maybe you play the victim, rescuer or perpetrator in your stories. Maybe you forever wander, never finding fulfillment of the desires you seek.

3. Today you have another story to tell. Not long ago your luminous warrior set out on a journey with good intention, a journey to discover your self, the most courageous journey of all. This is the story you are about to tell. This is your story of courage, your story of vision and quest, your story of intention, your story of darkness, your story of light. This is the story of your luminous warrior, for it is that longing of your soul that set you forth.

4. On the following page, you will write your story of this journey. Reflect back on your intention, meeting your Spirit ally, the insights and awareness, the struggles, the resistance, the breakthroughs, the fears. Let the story of your courageous journey be told, the story that is yours, and yours alone to tell, the one that can only be told by you. And don't even think about not being a writer!

5. List 5 things you are grateful for today.

Once upon a time, not long ago, my luminous warrior set out on a journey with good intention.

CEREMONY

"The only journey is the journey within."
RAINER MARIA RILKE

1. As part of your daily practice, follow *Letting Go of Expectations.* Notice what stood out or seemed significant. Write that here.

2. Through ceremony you step out of ordinary, linear reality and into the sacred dimension of timelessness. This realm is a powerful and profound space for communication with the Divine. Here your prayers enter the infinite matrix of mystical consciousness and your intentions are set in motion.

3. Your journey through this journal will culminate with a ceremonial prayer bundle, the despacho. For thousands of years, shamans of the Andes have worked with the Earth, the Mountains and the Spirit world for balance and ayni through this ceremony. A despacho is your gift to Spirit, a magical offering of your heart as it moves your intentions from the invisible energetic realms, to the visible realms of matter through its symbolic creation. The offerings of your despacho are placed in tissue or wrapping paper, tied up like a gift and offered to Spirit by return to the elements.

4. There are so many testaments to the power and effectiveness of this ancient ceremony in my life. Do not dismiss this part of your journey as unnecessary or frivolous. The work you have been doing until now has been in preparation for this ceremony and as such, the creation of your despacho is vital. You will need 30 to 45 minutes of solitude to complete this ceremony so if you are not able to create the time and space for that today, note when you will be able to do this in the next few days.

5. You will need the following items from this journal:

   - your Dear Fear letter

   - your Dear Diary entry

   - the story of your luminous warrior

   - any papers that were placed on your altar during this journal process

6. Other items you will need:

   - wrapping paper (non foil) or a few sheets of tissue paper

   - organic sugar

   - flower petals, bay leaves or small native leaves to create qintus to blow your prayers into (at least 36 leaves in total, enough to make 12 qintus)

   - offerings such as herbs, tobacco, incense, sweets, nuts, grains, spices, cocoa powder, dried fruits, sage

   - gold and silver threads and/or stars or confetti (can be found in craft stores)

   - glitter or sparkles

   - ribbon or string to tie your despacho

   - a flower, stick, twig or small branch for the outside of your despacho

7. You are creating sacred space in creating ceremony. Find a space free from clutter. Sit on the ground, or as close to the Earth as possible, as you lay your paper, and all the items you need, on the floor, or ground if you are working outside.

8. Start your ceremony with a prayer. Thank Pachamama for all she has provided in your life. Let her know you come before her in ceremony with your intention to restore right relationship, harmony and balance in your life. Ask for her help in releasing everything that gets in the way of your becoming, everything that gets in the way of your spiritual evolution. Ask for her help in releasing all lack and limitation, helping you to move from darkness to light. Call to the sacred mountains and oceans to hear your prayers and guide and illuminate your path. Call to your Spirit ally to be with you in ceremony for guidance and assistance. Call to the ancestors of this lineage of Earthkeepers who have made this ceremony available to us. Call to Divine Wisdom and Intelligence with any name and in any way that feels authentic to you. You can use song, shake a rattle, drum, light a candle, burn incense or sage, anything that helps you feel you are creating a time and space that feels sacred.

9. If you have never created a ceremony before, trust that your heart and soul know this way, for it is this part of you that comes to ceremony. You may be so accustomed to operating from your mind that ceremony might feel awkward. That is OK. Don't worry about whether you are doing something right or not. Trust in your sacred intuitive wisdom.

10. The creation of a despacho is done with focused intention. Everything that is placed in your despacho is done so with intent. Once you have your paper laid out you will create a bed for your prayers to lie on. First, place your letters and story from the journal in the center of the paper. Do so with a sense of gratitude, holding appreciation for the insights and awareness that have been revealed to you, the understandings you have come to know and all that remains a mystery. Next, designate a square in the center of the paper by placing organic sugar in your despacho to hold your intentions in sweetness. You can also add incense or sage here to clear the path for your prayers. Let this mark the heart of your despacho. Let your despacho hold everything from your journey of intention here.

11. You are now ready to add your prayers. Traditionally, three cocoa leaves are used to make a qintu to hold the energetic essence of your prayers by blowing them in with your breath. You can use bay leaves, which are just about the same size as a cocoa leaf, a small native leaf, or flower petals. Use three leaves or flower petals at a time and blow in your prayers, the same way you did for your Earth prayers.

12. Always let your first prayer be one of thanks to Mother Earth. Let your next qintu be a prayer of gratitude to the ancestors of this lineage of Earthkeepers that have shared this ancient wisdom and to the ancestors of your own lineage and family. Use the rest of your leaves or petals, at least 10 more qintus, to blow in your intention, blow in what you want to call into your life, blow in what you are ready to let go of and release, blow in prayers for your healing, for the healing of others. Once this process starts, you may find prayers arise you had not known were there before. Continue until you have used the rest of your qintus, even if it feels as if there are no more prayers left. Notice what it is like to be at an edge in prayer, to pray beyond the point where you feel you can no longer pray.

13. Once you blow your prayer into a qintu, place it in your despacho on top of the papers and sugar. Rather than drop it haphazardly, place your qintu with care, creating a pattern, allowing your intuition to guide the shape and form that appears. Trust your wisdom. Let beauty unfold. What is created is unique to you.

14. Once your qintus have been arranged in your despacho, you will feed your prayers with your offerings. Do so with a sense of gratitude and appreciation. Blow in a prayer of thanks to each of your offerings before you place them in your despacho. Rice and grains provide sustenance and fertility. Sage, incense and tobacco help carry your prayers to Spirit. Gold and silver items link your prayers to the sacred feminine and masculine, threads to the Moon, Sun and Stars. Flowers offer healing. Glitter adds color and vitality to your intentions. Chocolate honors this lineage and is loved by Pachamama. These are some of the intentions held with your offerings. If you add other items, do so with gratitude and intent.

15. Once your despacho is complete, place your hands just above it and feel the pulsing aliveness of your offering. Sense the vitality of the energy held within this sacred expression of your prayers. Closing your eyes can help heighten your sensitivity to feeling this energetic dimension.

16. Your despacho is now ready to be wrapped. Fold the bottom side up and the top side down so they cover your despacho. Now fold the right side in, then left over right so your entire despacho is covered in the shape of a square. Tie up your despacho with twine, ribbon or string, securing it on all four sides. Take care not to overturn your despacho to keep your prayers undisturbed.

17. On the outside of your despacho, tie a flower, stick, twig, or small branch into which you blow the intention of holding any forgotten prayers or intention.

18. Within the next three days you will need to offer your despacho back to the elements, letting go of any attachments to your prayers and intentions. You can bury your despacho in the Earth. The element of Earth will energetically compost your prayers and lay a solid foundation for your intentions. The element of fire creates a quick transformation so if you are able, you can burn your despacho in a fireplace, outdoor grill or firepit. It must completely burn to ash so make sure your fire is strong enough. You can also release your despacho into a natural body of water allowing the element of water to restore flow where you may be energetically stuck or stagnant. You can call on your Spirit ally to ask what is the best way to offer your despacho.

19. Notice your attachments to releasing your despacho. Notice attachments to releasing your letters from this journal. Watch how easily we become attached to papers or things, how difficult it can be to let go. When we see our resistance in releasing small things in our life,

we come to appreciate and honor the process of letting go of the larger beliefs and ideas that we hold on to, that define us and make us right, or justify our position. Letting go is essential to create the space and room for your desired intention to unfold.

20. List 5 things you are grateful for today.

*"If we could see the miracle of
a single flower clearly,*

our whole life would change."

BUDDHA

REFLECTIONS

"What progress, you ask, have I made?
I have begun to be a friend to myself."
HECATO

1. As part of your daily practice, choose a track to listen to today. Notice what stood out or seemed significant. Write that here.

2. Honor the commitment you have made to this path and the courage required to look within. I hope through this time you have come to befriend your soul. Reflect on your journal from the beginning. Feel the investment of your time and energy. Notice what stood out, what seemed most significant from this journey? Write that here.

3. What did you learn or notice about yourself through this process? What patterns emerged? What surprised you?

4. What was difficult or most challenging for you?

5. Notice how you approached this journal. Did you start with much enthusiasm and then fade? Were you skeptical? Did you read the entire book first feeling you needed to know everything before you started? Did you put little effort in expecting big results? Did you procrastinate along the way? Did you feel like you knew everything already? How does your approach to this journal show up in how you approach other aspects of your life?

6. When you were called to action, were you able to follow through? If not, what prevented you or got in the way? How do these patterns show up in other aspects of your life?

7. Where are you now regarding your intention? What has manifested as a result of your intention? What inspirations have you received? What, if anything, has shifted? Has your intention changed from when you started?

8. What wisdom have you gained?

9. What would you like to acknowledge about yourself through this journey? Create a positive statement about yourself, in the present tense, and write that here.

10. What is one thing you can do that will continue to support you on a daily basis? Write that here.

11. Bring your hands together in front of your heart in a prayer position as you bow to honor the gift that you are to this world.

With deep gratitude I thank you,

from the depth of my heart,

for your leap of faith

in investing your time and energy in this journal.

I honor your courage and willingness

to consciously create a life of higher purpose and meaning,

for yourself,

and for the world in which we share.

~NAMASTE~

NOTES

Afterword

How lovely would it be to offer wisdom from the perspective of an enlightened childhood, a life full of healthy relationships, a path graced with ease and insight. These, however, are not the circumstances from which wisdom arose. Wisdom was born through wounds and demons, facing fear and finding liberation, trusting mystery and finding magic, born from heeding the call of Spirit.

Wisdom lays before us when we follow a path illuminated by others, however that wisdom is not our own until it is woven into our soul. For wisdom to reach deep in your marrow you must walk a path uniquely alone. You must listen to the voice that calls from within, even when that voice defies all reason. To stand in your truth, the truth as you know it, regardless if anyone believes it is true, this is the wisdom that sources from power. This is the wisdom residing in you.

My first steps on a healing path came in 1985 as I entered school for Physical Therapy. Although my intention was to find a job with security, my body was desperate in its cry for healing. I had started smoking at 11 years old. Fifteen years later, as I entered PT school, my habit was up to two packs a day. Stepping into a field of health and healing was the spark that spurred the success to quit. How could I help others heal their body, if I could not help myself? Not only did I quit, but the body I had suffocated with smoke and nicotine went on to run the NYC marathon in 3 1/2 hours just a few years later. The healing wisdom of the body awakened my path.

In the early days of my career, I saw people with injuries in their body believing the problem to be in the joint or muscle that was causing the pain. With time, evolution and countless studies in Eastern and Western medicine ways, it became clear. Pain is a wake up call, a cry from the body to pay attention to something deeper. It is that something deeper I have dedicated my life to. It is that something deeper that keeps inspiring me on a healing path. It is that something deeper that calls to my soul.

The first incarnation of this journal was written five years ago, with the title *"Success Journal: Daily Practices to Help Manifest Your Intentions"*. Although a template was laid then, the years were essential for the evolution of this work. I see the necessity of time to ready this journal, and myself, for its birth. As with every birth, this one was not free from pain and suffering.

Although there are many places in my life I can point to with success, it is the path of intimacy where I have suffered the most. From the longing to be loved by a father lost to alcohol, to promiscuity in my days of youth, to the pain of divorce and shattered illusions, followed by non-sustainable love affairs with unavailable men, intimate relationship is where I feel I have failed miserably. Through the path of intimacy come my deepest cries to heal. It is the path of intimacy that holds the deepest wounds to my soul.

After yet another relationship in my life dismantled, events unfolded, providing a mirror, where I could bear witness to the darkness within. The words, *I am not*, arising from shadows, tormented me with the judgment, *I do not exist*. This voice that informed me, *I am not enough*, became the fundamental belief through which I struggled to find intimacy. This wound imprinted itself before cognition; encoding my being with the fear of nonexistence. This unrelenting decree, *I am not*, created the heart wrenching pain in every intimate connection, including the one with my very own soul.

For if in the teachings of Moses, the name of God is *I Am*, then the words *I Am Not* means God is not. The voice that informs me says *I am not God*. Stepping into the pain that I do not exist was an identity crisis of my most essential essence; an identity crisis of Spirit. So the painful question arose, if God is *I Am,* and *I am not,* then *who am I?*

Who am I?

This question arises in response to many facets of our identity. When the question arose from a query of my own existence, the identity crisis became one of my soul. In entering an identity crisis of Spirit, solace is not found in human contact. There are no words of wisdom to rescue one from the place of painful isolation that marks this dark night of the soul. A hug or warm embrace is no condolence. With nowhere to turn in my isolating loneliness, left wounded again from the loss of a lover, my pain and grief led me into the woods.

It was here, in communion with Mother Earth, I was cradled in comfort. Walking barefoot on her bountiful grounds, purified in her salt waters, cleansed by her fierce winds, I discovered the voice I am. I found myself in the home of belonging. From this Spirit restoration, wisdom was born. Although I practiced and studied for decades, the loneliest despair bore the truth of this knowing, the teachings of Earth woven into my soul.

Although the practices in this book span the wisdom of history and culture, many arose from time in the woods. They are the benevolent calling of Pachamama to each one of us as sons and daughters of the Earth. I offer them to you, as they have been offered to me, for healing, awareness, transformation and wisdom.

With reverence and awe, I heed this call.

About the Author

Karen Chrappa, a holistic physiotherapist in practice 25 years has worked with thousands of people on a healing path. Her work weaves together an intuitive tapestry of medicine paths from a lifetime of dedicated studies in contemporary and indigenous ways. She continues to deepen her own spiritual evolution working with shamans in Peru to awaken the Sacred Feminine as part of the ayllu a Bouquet of Light. She currently lives on Long Island, NY with her two teenage daughters. Visit online at www.karenchrappa.com

Glossary

<u>Aho</u> - exaltation meaning victory to Spirit.

<u>Archetype</u> - According to Jung, archetypes are psychological patterns, operating through the psyche, that are unique to an individual yet arise from a universal, historical and collective consciousness.

<u>Apus</u> - Incan and Andean word for mountains, worshiped and revered for the sacred wisdom they embody.

<u>Ayllu</u> - tribe.

<u>Ayni</u> - being in "right relationship", including the relationship with our own heart, with others and with Nature. Ayni indicates a reciprocity and mutual exchange in relationship, a balance between giving and receiving.

<u>Chakra</u> - Sanskrit word meaning wheels of light. Energetic vortexes that connect the luminous energy body to the physical body. Seven main chakras are located along the spine. Shamans traditionally work with three; at the heart, belly and third eye.

<u>Despacho</u> - a ceremonial prayer bundle of the Andes for healing, to restore ayni, to bring oneself back into alignment with Nature, Spirit and destiny.

<u>Hucha</u> - dark, heavy, dense energies in the luminous body.

<u>Limpias</u> - spiritual cleansing using plants, flowers, herbs or eggs.

<u>Luminous Body</u> - the electromagnetic field that surrounds the physical body, also referred to as the light body, or aura. The luminous body is the template that informs and shapes the physical body by the darkness and light emanating through its field, reflecting thought, unresolved emotion, wounds, trauma, ancestral patterns and beliefs that can dim the light of this luminous electromagnetic body.

<u>Mantra</u> - sacred sounds used to invoke higher states of consciousness through repetition of chanting or speaking, either silently, or out loud.

<u>Namaste</u> - a Sanskrit word meaning I honor the light in you that is also in me.

<u>Pachamama</u> - Incan name for Mother Earth.

Qintu - a prayer holder in Peru made from three cocoa leaves. Prayers are transferred to the leaves by blowing them in with your breath.

Shaman - medicine men and women who work with Energy, Nature, the elements and the Spirit world to restore balance and harmony for individuals, communities and the world at large, working through prayer, ceremony and intention.

Shamanic Journey - an ancient and indigenous practice used by shamans to receive information from the Spirit world with a specific intention.

Spirit Ally - a guide to assist your soul on its path of destiny with information from sacred and mythic realms.

Third Eye - sixth chakra located at the center of the forehead where psychic power and intuition reside.

Resources

Readings to Further Your Journey:

Arvigo, Rosita, and Nadine Epstein. *Spiritual Bathing: Healing Rituals and Traditions from around the World*. Berkeley, CA: Celestial Arts, 2003. Print.

Barks, Coleman. *The Essential Rumi*. San Francisco, CA: Harper, 1995. Print.

Barks, Coleman, and Michael Green. *The Illuminated Rumi*. New York: Broadway, 1997. Print.

Braden, Gregg. *Secrets of the Lost Mode of Prayer: the Hidden Power of Beauty, Blessing, Wisdom, and Hurt*. Carlsbad, CA: Hay House, 2006. Print.

Carnes, Robin, and Sally Craig. *Sacred Circles: a Guide to Creating Your Own Women's Spirituality Group*. San Francisco: HarperSanFrancisco, 1998. Print.

Chodron, Pema. *When Things Fall Apart: Heart Advice for Difficult times*. Boston: Shambhala, 1997. Print.

Cope, Stephen. *Yoga and the Quest for the True Self*. New York: Bantam, 1999. Print.

Deida, David. *Blue Truth: a Spiritual Guide to Life & Death and Love & Sex*. [S.l.]: Read How You Want, 2009. Print.

Farmer, Steven. *Sacred Ceremony: How to Create Ceremonies for Healing, Transitions, and Celebrations*. Carlsbad, CA: Hay House, 2002. Print.

Kabat-Zinn, Jon. *Wherever You Go, There You Are: Mindfulness Meditation in Everyday Life*. New York: Hyperion, 1994. Print.

Levine, Stephen. *A Gradual Awakening*. New York: Anchor, 1989. Print.Levine, Stephen, A Gradual Awakening

Lipsey, Stefanie. *Sound Cliff: Twelve Words to a More Creative Life; Poem Collages with Weekly Exercises*. Scotts Valley, CA: CreateSpace, 2009.

Moore, Thomas. *Care of the Soul: a Guide for Cultivating Depth and Sacredness in Everyday Life*. New York, NY: HarperCollins, 1992. Print.

Myss, Caroline M. *Defy Gravity: Healing beyond the Bounds of Reason*. Carlsbad, CA: Hay House, 2009. Print.

Myss, Caroline M. *Sacred Contracts: Awakening Your Divine Potential*. New York: Harmony, 2001. Print.

Osho. *Love, Freedom, Aloneness: the Koan of Relationships*. New York: St. Martin's Griffin, 2001. Print.

Peck, M. Scott. *The Road Less Traveled: a New Psychology of Love, Traditional Values, and Spiritual Growth*. New York: Simon and Schuster, 1978. Print.

Streep, Peg. *Spiritual Gardening: Creating Sacred Space Outdoors*. Alexandria, VA: Time-Life, 1999.

Scheffel, Bill. *Loving-kindness Meditation: Meditations to Help You Love Yourself, Love Others, and Create More Love and Peace in the World*. Gloucester, MA: Fair Winds, 2003. Print.

Suzuki, Shunryu. *Zen Mind, Beginner's Mind*. New York: Walker/Weatherhill, 1970. Print.

Villoldo, Alberto. *Courageous Dreaming: How Shamans Dream the World into Being*. Carlsbad, CA: Hay House, 2008. Print.

Villoldo, Alberto. *Mending the past and Healing the Future with Soul Retrieval*. Carlsbad, CA: Hay House, 2005. Print.

Villoldo, Alberto. *Shaman, Healer, Sage: How to Heal Yourself and Others with the Energy Medicine of the Americas*. New York: Harmony, 2000. Print.

Wilber, Ken. *Grace and Grit: Spirituality and Healing in the Life and Death of Treya Killam Wilber*. Boston: Shambhala, 1991. Print.

Informative and Enlightening Websites:

EFTUniverse.com. Web. 24 Jan. 2011. http://www.eftuniverse.com.

Jung, Carl. "Jung's Archetypes." Iloveulove.com - Unconditional Love, Forgiveness, Relationships, Love & Spirituality. Books, Articles, Advice, Forums. Web. 29 Jan. 2011. http://www.iloveulove. com/psychology/jung/jungarchetypes.html.

Kristin Fontana, Evolutionary Astrologer. Web. 24 Jan. 2011. http://www.kristinfontana.com.

"Hidden Chapel Studios | Facebook." Welcome to Facebook. Web. 24 Jan. 2011. http://www. facebook.com/pages/Hidden-Chapel-Studios/234618627668.

Rainbow Jaguar. Web. 24 Jan. 2011. http://www.rainbowjaguar.org.

"Royalty Free Music." Incompetech. Web. 24 Jan. 2011. http://incompetech.com/m/c/royalty-free.

Shamans Supplies by Shamans Market. Web. 24 Jan. 2011. http://www.shamansmarket.com.

The Four Winds Society - Healing the Light Body School and Peru Expeditions. Web. 24 Jan. 2011. http://www.thefourwinds.com.

Western Mountain. Web. 24 Jan. 2011. http://westernmountain.org.

Shamanic Prayer Bundles. Web. 24 Jan. 2011. http://www.prayerbundles.com.